Primary S̶ ̶ ̶ ̶ ̶ ̶ e
National Curriculum

Primary Special Needs and the National Curriculum

Second edition

Ann Lewis

London and New York

First published 1991
by Routledge
11 New Fetter Lane, London EC4P 4EE

Reprinted 1992 and 1993
Second edition published 1995
by Routledge

Simultaneously published in the USA and Canada
by Routledge
29 West 35th Street, New York, NY 10001

© 1991, 1995 Ann Lewis

Typeset in Palatino by
Ponting–Green Publishing Services, Chesham, Bucks
Printed and bound in Great Britain by
T.J. Press (Padstow) Ltd, Padstow, Cornwall

British Library Cataloguing in Publication Data
A catalogue record for this book is available from the
British Library

Library of Congress Cataloguing in Publication Data
A catalogue record for this book has been requested

ISBN   0–415–12582–0

Contents

Figures and tables

FIGURES

TABLES

Acknowledgements

Many people have contributed indirectly to this book and my thanks go to them all. The ideas have been shaped by the multifarious children, students and colleagues with whom I have worked in London, the West Midlands and the USA. My thanks in particular to Jim Campbell, Tricia David, Anne Sinclair-Taylor, Lois Thorpe and Liz Waine who have commented incisively on draft material. Reactions, from reviewers and other readers, to the first edition have influenced the foci of this version. My apologies to the teacher who sent me the photograph of herself reading the book on a beach in Barbados for not including her photograph in this edition. I am grateful to Simon for permission to include copies of his 'Fairy Liquid' writing and to the DFE for clarification concerning regulations for temporary exceptions. At Routledge, Helen Fairlie and Sam Larkham have continued to provide valued and good-humoured editorial support.

My special thanks to Gerry for his tolerance, continuing encouragement and constructive comments on draft material.

Extracts from Chapter 1 have been published in *Education 3–13* (volume 23, number 1, pp. 13–18) or the *British Journal of Educational Studies* (volume 43, number 3) and are reproduced with the permission of the respective editors. Part of Chapter 8 was published in *Special Children* and is included here with the permission of Howard Sharron.

Abbreviations

ATL	Asssociation of Teachers and Lecturers
CACE	Central Advisory Council for Education
CATS	Consortium for Assessment and Testing in Schools
DES	Department of Education and Science
DFE	Department for Education
GEST	Grants for Education Support and Training
HMI	Her Majesty's Inspectorate (of schools)
INSET	In-service Education of Teachers
NASEN	National Association for Special Educational Needs
NCET	National Council for Educational Technology
NFER	National Foundation for Educational Research
OFSTED	Office for Standards in Education
PACE	Primary Assessment and Curriculum Experience
PMLD	Profound and Multiple Learning Difficulties
PoS	Programme of Study
RNIB	Royal National Institute for the Blind
RNID	Royal National Institute for the Deaf
SATs	Standard Assessment Tasks
SCAA	School Curriculum and Assessment Authority
SEAC	School Examinations and Assessment Council
SENCO	Special Educational Needs Coordinator
SEN	Special Educational Needs
SLD	Severe Learning Difficulties
STAIR	Standard Tests and Assessment Implementation Research
STs	Standard Tasks
TGAT	Task Group on Assessment and Testing

Chapter 1

The story so far

The aim of this book is to address the issues and practicalities of implementing the National Curriculum at classroom level in mainstream primary schools. The approach is pragmatic: we have a National Curriculum and we must use it to foster progress for children who find school-based learning difficult. Some of these children may have statements of special educational needs but most are likely to be without the protection, or millstone, depending on one's ideological stance, of a statement.

The National Curriculum is a statement of educational entitlement to which no child should be denied. To withdraw a child's entitlement by disapplying the National Curriculum requires strong justification. There is, despite some initial confusion, no ambiguity in the various National Curriculum documents about the broad situation for children with special educational needs. These children, if they are in maintained schools, should participate in the National Curriculum. It is not the case, as has been reported incorrectly, that the National Curriculum is automatically disapplied for all children with statements or for children attending special schools. The Code of Practice on special educational needs (DFE 1994a) reiterates the inclusivity of the National Curriculum: 'Children with special educational needs require the greatest possible degree of access to a broad and balanced curriculum including the National Curriculum' (para. 1. 2).

This chapter begins with a brief discussion about the nature of special educational needs. This is followed by a review of evidence about the impact of the National Curriculum on children with special educational needs. Then six recent shifts in thinking concerning provision for children with special educational needs are discussed. These are related, first, to the 1994–5 revisions to the National Curriculum and, second, to the Code of Practice on the identification and assessment of special educational needs (DFE 1994a). This material sets the scene for the following chapters which examine directly the classroom implementation of the National Curriculum.

NATURE OF SPECIAL EDUCATIONAL NEEDS

This book is about adapting and developing the National Curriculum for children who experience difficulties in school-based learning. Difficulties in learning may stem from factors within the child, such as poor short-term memory, and/or from a mismatch between the learning opportunities which children need and the educational experiences which are being provided. This stance is reflected in the National Curriculum Council's (1989a) statement that, 'Special educational needs are not just a reflection of pupils' inherent difficulties or disabilities; they are often related to factors within schools which can prevent or exacerbate problems' (para. 5). This statement stresses that special educational needs are not purely within the child. A child's special educational needs may be more or less problematic for the teacher, depending on the ways in which the school responds to the child.

This stance was also evident in the report by the House of Commons Select Committee on statements of special educational needs (House of Commons 1993). This report noted that three views were expressed very strongly by many witnesses. These views were that:

1 the more effective the provision made by mainstream schools for less severe special needs, the smaller the number of children referred for statutory assessment (i.e. statements);
2 the better mainstream schools are resourced, the smaller the number of special needs that arise;
3 the more effective the support services available to main-stream schools, the smaller the number of children requiring statements.

In other words, special needs are directly related to provision. The same emphasis, that special needs may be compounded, or caused, by the educational provision received by the child, is central to the Code of Practice. This is made explicit:

> Schools should not automatically assume that children's learning difficulties always result solely or even mainly from problems within the child. The school's practices can make a difference – for good or ill.

(DFE 1994a: para. 2.19)

The requirements of children with special educational needs are one element within overall planning in the school. Special needs provision is likely to be more effective if the concern about providing for children with special educational needs runs through all documents than if it is considered only in separate policy documents. A fruitful approach is to think about how the school promotes the differentiation of the curriculum, rather than identifying children with special educational needs as a particular group. There is a danger that, by focusing specifically on children with special educational needs, they become seen as invariably needing something different from other children. What is needed is the recognition and acceptance of individuality applied to all children.

Many researchers have tried to identify whether or not children who have difficulties in school-based learning are different from other children in terms of effective teaching approaches. It has been asked whether these children are just 'delayed' or qualitatively 'different' from other children in the ways in which they learn. This is an important question for teachers. Should a 9-year-old with reading difficulties, reading at the level of a typical 7-year-old, be taught in the same way as normal 7-year-olds? To answer 'yes' to this question would be to imply that the first child is delayed but not qualitatively different in his or her learning needs from those of the second child.

The evidence from both practice and research is that, unsurprisingly, children with learning difficulties are a heterogeneous group. An extensive review of research on learner and teacher characteristics (Cronbach and Snow 1977) concluded that it is impossible to make firm generalisations about certain teaching methods being more effective than others for 'low ability' children. There was, for example, no support for teaching children with learning difficulties solely through a didactic, step-by-step method. However, the review did provide qualified support for the view that children with learning difficulties benefit more from didactic methods than from guided learning whereas the reverse tends to be the case for able children. The implication is that children with difficulties in learning need a mixture of teaching approaches with a bias towards fairly structured methods.

One reason for the failure of research to come up with 'best buys' in terms of teaching methods specifically orientated to children with difficulties in learning, as a group, is the heterogeneity of that group. One broad theoretical distinction within the group has been between children who are generally 'slow' compared with peers, and children who have a specific learning difficulty in one or several areas but otherwise have average or above-average attainments compared with peers (Rutter and Yule 1975). A detailed analysis and critique of research into children with reading difficulties concluded that the research literature provided no support for the idea that there is a need for a scientific concept of dyslexia separate from other, more neutral terms, such as 'poor reader' (Stanovitch 1994). Work over the last decade has endeavoured to identify specific subgroups of reading difficulties and there is evidence that it may be valid to distinguish between children with language, visual-spatial, or 'mixed processing deficits' (Tyler 1990). (See Adams (1990) for a comprehensive review of research into beginning reading.) However, even if we could make these kinds of distinction with certainty, there remains the question of how best to teach these various groups of children. As yet there are no unequivocally 'best' methods based on specific diagnoses. Carol Aubrey (1993) reviewing research into teaching in special education noted that:

> Such children [with mild handicapping conditions] do not require a special or different curriculum nor do they need special or different teaching. They may need more and better ... 'high density' education but not a qualitatively different kind of education.
>
> (Aubrey 1993: 15)

Flexibility in teaching methods, careful monitoring of the child's learning, and the encouragement of a broad range of learning strategies remain important characteristics of effective teaching for all children.

EVIDENCE ABOUT THE IMPACT OF THE NATIONAL CURRICULUM ON CHILDREN WITH SPECIAL EDUCATIONAL NEEDS

There were many reservations at the consultation stage about the suitability and practicability of the proposed National Curriculum in relation to children with special educational needs (Haviland 1988, Simon 1988, Kelly 1990, Wedell 1990). These reservations centred on two areas in particular. First, there were concerns that schools, with an eye on test scores, would not want to admit, or to retain, children who might lower the school's results. Second, the narrowness of the prescribed National Curriculum was seen as disadvantageous to, and inappropriate for, many children with special educational needs. The National Curriculum and other aspects of the 1988 Education Act were seen as ideologically in conflict with the 1981 Education Act (Lloyd-Smith 1992) These arguments were developed and, to some extent, the reservations confirmed, as the National Curriculum began to be implemented.

Since the first edition of this book was published (in 1991), at a time when the National Curriculum was just coming on stream, there has been extensive evidence to show that teachers in mainstream schools are generally supportive of the National Curriculum framework, including its suitability for children with special educational needs (SCAA 1994a). Research into the implementation of the National Curriculum in special schools has shown that even there, few children have been taken out of the National Curriculum (Lewis and Halpin 1994). Teachers have made determined efforts to show that virtually all children can participate in the National Curriculum. A national survey of nearly 300 mainstream primary schools found that over 90 per cent of the schools surveyed included in National Curriculum programmes, as a matter of policy, all children with special educational needs (Lewis 1995a). Although these teachers were aiming to include children with special educational needs in the National Curriculum, there was also a great deal of ambivalence about doing so. Thirty-seven per cent of the respondents concluded that on balance the National Curriculum was a good thing for children with special educational needs, 14 per cent that it was not a good thing and 46 per cent that it was partly a good thing. This ambivalence is reflected in the wider picture of perceived strengths and difficulties in the implementation of the National Curriculum for children with special educational needs.

Reported benefits of the National Curriculum for children with special educational needs

A wide range of benefits of the National Curriculum for children with special educational needs have been reported by mainstream primary teachers (Lewis 1995a). The three most frequently cited benefits were (a) the provision to all children of the same basic educational entitlement (b) a clear curricular framework and (c) a structure within which to differentiate learning for pupils with special educational needs. About one respondent in ten mentioned one or more of these points as being a particular benefit for pupils with special needs in their schools. These findings reflect perceptions and we cannot know from these data the effects on practice. However a succession of surveys, notably by HMI, support claimed benefits of the National Curriculum for children with special needs. In particular, it has been reported that after the introduction of the National Curriculum children with special needs experienced greater curricular coherence, raised teacher expectations, broader curricula, improved assessment and better record keeping (DES 1990a, 1991a). There have also been claims of greater consistency between special and mainstream school practice (in effect, that special schools became more like mainstream schools); this has been interpreted as beneficial.

It is clear that teachers have been putting in a vast amount of time to implement the National Curriculum. Typically, teachers in primary schools (1990–1) were working between 50 and 55 hours each week in term time (Campbell and Neill 1994). Similar surveys have produced comparable findings (Coopers and Lybrand Deloitte 1991, Lowe 1991, NAS/UWT 1991, Osborn and Black 1994). Most of this work overload was in teachers' own time as work associated with teaching spilled into evenings and weekends. The long working week (compared with previous data for teaching and with many other occupational groups) was not a temporary blip due only to the introduction of the National Curriculum: 'Something like a 50 hour working week looks established as a permanent feature of primary teaching in the 1990s' (Campbell and Neill 1994: 162). Time demands were not only extensive, but also intensive. There was much simultaneous working leading to feelings of working harder but achieving less. The researchers noted the pervasive influence of teachers' sense of 'conscientiousness'. Teachers were reducing their own educational objectives in order to meet (different) governmental objectives. The teachers were 'trapped by their own conscientiousness' (Campbell and Neill 1994: 223).

Reported reservations about, and problems in, the National Curriculum for children with special educational needs

Teachers' support for the National Curriculum in principle for children with special needs has gone alongside some reservations about it in practice. One might anticipate that if the National Curriculum is inappropriate for children with special needs then this would be particularly evident in special schools. Within this educational sector there have been divided views about the value of the National Curriculum for those pupils (for example, Daniels and Ware 1990, Sebba et al. 1993, Ashdown et al. 1991). These contrasting views have appeared most strongly in relation to pupils with severe or profound learning difficulties. Sue Fagg, Judy Sebba and their co-workers (Fagg et al. 1990, Sebba et al. 1993) have held that the National Curriculum has been a useful antidote to a narrowing of special school curricula and that it has promoted links between special and mainstream schools. However, other analysts, such as John White (1991), suggest that the National Curriculum is fundamentally irrelevant to many pupils, particularly those for whom schools exercise a duty of care, rather than education.

These divergent views are interesting because they have prompted a broader debate about what it is that is special about special education, whether that takes place in mainstream or in special schools. There can be no single right answer to this question, the nature of the 'specialness' of special education will vary for individuals. However, probing responses to the question is important because, as Brahm Norwich has pointed out (1994a), this highlights tensions and ambivalence among those working with children with special needs. In particular, it is becoming clear that contrasting reactions to the National Curriculum reflect these different underlying value positions, characterised by an emphasis on equality of educational opportunities (give all children similar opportunities) or individuality (individualise opportunities). This issue is taken up again in Chapter 5.

Mainstream primary schools have also reported a wide range of disadvantages of the National Curriculum for children with special educational needs. In the survey of mainstream primary schools referred to earlier (Lewis 1995a) the most frequently cited disadvantages of the National Curriculum for children with special educational needs were: problems in effectively differentiating the curriculum (mentioned by approximately one school in six), providing the breadth of curriculum without sacrificing depth, and having inadequate resources to fulfil curricular demands. The last two points were raised as difficulties by about one school in ten.

Perceptions of the curriculum are, as newly trained teachers move into mainstream primary schools, decreasingly influenced by experience of teaching pre-National Curriculum curricula. The task now is to build constructively on experience of the National Curriculum in order to capitalise on its recognised strengths and to remove, or at least to diminish, its disadvantages.

THE NEW CONTEXT: A REVISED NATIONAL CURRICULUM AND THE CODE OF PRACTICE

During 1993 and 1994 there was a plethora of documents from the Department for Education (DFE) related to provision for children with special educational needs in mainstream schools. Over 26 consultation papers and draft or final versions of circulars and regulations on this topic were published in the nine months between September 1993 and May 1994. So the situation concerning mainstream special needs has been changing, and will continue to change, as this series of documents takes effect. The most significant changes are likely to be as a result of changes to the National Curriculum (DFE 1995) alongside the introduction of the Code of Practice (DFE 1994a).

The revised National Curriculum (DFE 1995) increases the flexibility of the National Curriculum in four main ways. First, programmes of study mention the possibility of using communication (other than conventional written language) to convey responses or to give a child access to a task. This opens up conventional reading and writing tasks to a wider group of children including those who could carry out the tasks success-

fully using microcomputer support. Second, ages and programmes of study have been unlinked so that children can work
on material appropriate to their developmental levels, regardless
of the National Curriculum level or key stage to which that
material is notionally tied. Third, the overall reduction in curricular content creates a smaller amount of statutory studies.
This means that, potentially, children with learning difficulties
will not be pushed hastily through curricular content because this
is so vast that there is no time for consolidation. Fourth, there
is an explicit proportion of time (20 per cent) for a variety of non-
National Curriculum work. How schools use this time can be
decided on the basis of children's individual needs and school
priorities or strengths. This increased flexibility was signalled in
Ron Dearing's final report:

> It is impossible to prescribe a curriculum which will meet the
> needs of every pupil. What the National Curriculum should and
> must do is to allow teachers and schools to meet the particular
> needs of pupils with special educational needs in ways which
> they judge to be relevant
>
> (SCAA 1994b: 6.2)

This recognises the importance of teachers using their professional
judgements to adapt curricula to individual children's learning
needs. The revised National Curriculum, with its greater flexibility, has a stronger claim than earlier versions to be appropriate
for a broad range of children.

Increasing the flexibility in the National Curriculum has a useful
side-effect: a potential reduction in the need for statements. The
connection between demands for resources (reflected in statements) and the curriculum was made explicitly by the 1993 House
of Commons Select Committee:

> [The] demand for statements might be reduced . . . [by] a more
> sensitively differentiated delivery of the National Curriculum.
>
> (para. 33)

If teachers can routinely differentiate the curriculum, then there
is no case for additional resources to enable a child to access the
National Curriculum. If extra resources are not needed then, by
definition, there is no need for the child to be given a statement of
special needs. By implication, changes to the National Curriculum

that make it more flexible, and so inclusive of children with special needs, should also reduce the demand for statements.

At about the same time as these revisions to the National Curriculum, schools became subject to the Code of Practice on the identification and assessment of special educational needs (DFE 1994a). The Code proposed a five-stage procedure in which the first three stages of assessment and monitoring of a child's special needs are primarily the responsibility of the class teacher and the school's special needs coordinator. An extensive range of information is given as required at each stage (including curricular attainments, standardised test results, parental reports and the child's perceptions of his or her difficulties plus, at stages 2 and 3, an individual education plan). It is only after examination of the child's special needs has moved through three school-based stages that consideration of the need for a statement will be made. The orientation of the Code is very similar to that put forward in the 1985 Fish Report on special educational needs in inner London schools (ILEA 1985a). That report noted:

> Schools tend to regard the identification of children with special educational needs as tantamount to referring them for special educational provision, rather than seeing identification as the first stage of a process of experimental intervention in school which is carefully monitored.
>
> (ILEA 1985a: para. 58)

This comment crystallises the approach embodied in the Code of Practice. This emphasises procedures and provision within mainstream schools for children who have special educational needs but not statements of special need.

SHIFTS IN THINKING ABOUT SCHOOL-BASED PROVISION FOR CHILDREN WITH SPECIAL EDUCATIONAL NEEDS

The revisions to the National Curriculum and the introduction of the Code of Practice can be seen as crystallising some important shifts in thinking about the education of children with special educational needs, especially those in mainstream schools. These shifts are:

- an emphasis on children with special needs but without statements,

- increasing prominence given to the role of the special educational needs coordinator,
- a re-focusing in the special needs infrastructure in schools and local education authorities,
- an increased stress on partnerships with parents,
- greater accountability concerning mainstream special needs provision, and
- a tightening of the legal framework.

Emphasis on children with special needs but without statements

Why has there been a shift away from children with statements and towards children with special needs but without statements? This shift reflects the way in which legislation and resources had come to be directed disproportionately towards children with statements. The 1981 Education Act established the roots of the present assessment procedures for children with special needs and, through the implementation of this Act, led to an emphasis on children with marked special needs, notionally the 2 per cent who had traditionally attended segregated special schooling. In summary, the 1981 Education Act assessment procedures set up a system whereby a subgroup of children with special needs was identified and the individual children issued with a statement of provision required to meet those needs. This statement was legally binding and so, at least in theory, guaranteed that the child's Local Education Authority provided what was specified.

During the 1980s there were increasing concerns about the way in which the 1981 Education Act was working. One concern reflected increasing numbers, and hence costs, of statements (Audit Commission/HMI 1992, House of Commons 1993, Audit Commission 1994). Statements as a way of obtaining scarce resources, parental pressures for statements, and the role of the National Curriculum in drawing teachers' attention to the different needs of a wide range of pupils (Lunt and Evans 1991) probably all played a part in leading to the issuing of more statements of special educational needs.

A second source of uneasiness has been the regional variations in numbers and ranges of children given statements (Audit Commission/HMI 1992, House of Commons 1993, Wedell 1993, Norwich 1994b). This variability has been cited repeatedly by government, parent and professional groups as a matter for concern. It has been seen as patently unfair that the level of provision received by a child should depend on the accident of where he or she attends school. The Code of Practice can be seen as an attempt to level some of these disparities.

Another concern, linked with rising numbers of statements, has been the widening groups of children being encompassed by statementing procedures (discussed in Lewis and Sammons 1994). This reflects a broadening of the basis on which statements have been issued. The proportion of children with statements of special needs who are in mainstream schools has increased substantially. In 1985 only 14 per cent of pupils with statements were in mainstream schools. Six years later this proportion had tripled and nearly half the pupils with statements (42 per cent) were in mainstream schools (OFSTED 1992). This increase contrasts with the implicit message in the DFE's updated parents' guide concerning children with special educational needs (DFE 1994b). This states that pupils in special schools will have statements but makes no mention of the fact that pupils in mainstream schools may also have statements. The growth in numbers of children in mainstream schools who have statements of special educational needs is not due to a large movement of pupils out of special and into mainstream schools. Between 1988 and 1991 there was only a small shift (of 8 per cent) towards 'integration' in terms of a decrease in the proportion of the school population in segregated provision (Swann 1992). There is also evidence that more recently this overall trend has been reversed and there has been, on balance, a small national increase in special school placements (Norwich 1994b). This supports the view that the groups of children now receiving statements have widened considerably beyond those for whom they were originally envisaged (i.e. the '2 per cent' attending special schools).

So for all these reasons there has developed a feeling among professionals, parents and government that the emphasis on statements as the main route to allocation of special needs resources was misguided and no longer effective or equitable. If resources for special needs are taken up by children with statements then children with special needs but without statements may lose out. Both the Code of Practice and changes to the National Curriculum (DFE 1995) can be seen as mechanisms to reduce the number and proportion of children with statements and also to emphasise and develop the quality of provision for the wider group of children with special educational needs (Lewis 1995b). These goals can be achieved by improving what is routinely provided for all children with special educational needs and so obviating the demand for a statement.

A group of children with special needs, most of whom do not have statements, but about whom there is increasing concern, are children excluded from mainstream schools. There has been a dramatic increase, particularly at primary level, in the number of permanent exclusions. OFSTED (1993a) noted 'This rise in exclusions is steady in most LEAs and dramatic in some with a noticeable increase in the number of pupils being excluded at primary age' (1993a: para. 7). The tone of circular 10/94 on exclusions (DFE 1994b) is integrationist in the sense that headteachers are urged not to reach too readily for exclusion as a way of responding to pupil behaviour. This inevitably raises issues about the nature of the mainstream curriculum for those children.

Increasing prominence given to the role of the special educational needs coordinator

If schools, parents and governors are to be convinced that they can meet children's special needs without recourse to statements then there is a need to increase the profile of special needs in mainstream schools. A central mechanism, described in detail in the Code, is that of the special needs coordinator. Ironically, the emphasis in the Code on the special needs coordinator may take attention away from the vital role of the class teacher in pre-emptively identifying and responding to children's special educational needs.

In the 1970s and early 1980s posts of responsibility in primary schools tended to be associated with curricular subjects, administration (such as responsibility for a broad age phase) or with a small number of generic areas (for example, home–school liaison). Special educational needs or 'remedial work' were uncommon as foci for specific posts of responsibility or incentive allowances (see, for example, DES 1978a, DES 1982a, Croll and Moses 1985). The Fish Report, in a recommendation that anticipated the Code of Practice nearly a decade later, recommended that:

[Some] teachers be designated and trained to be responsible for advice on special educational needs as well as class teaching responsibilities and to be a member of a group of similar curriculum leaders in larger primary schools or in a group of smaller primary schools, and that time be allocated for this work.

(ILEA 1985a: para. 3.17.22)

The role of special needs coordinator was stimulated by the findings of a survey by HMI which concluded that designated specialist coordinators for special educational needs were important contributors in almost all of the schools in which good practice was observed (DES 1989a). This survey reported that two-thirds of the primary schools visited had a member of staff with coordinating responsibility for special educational needs. These posts were probably not exclusively for special educational needs. Research carried out into the Primary Needs Programme in Leeds during 1986 and 1987 found that few primary school coordinators defined their roles purely in terms of special educational needs (Alexander *et al.* 1989). However three-quarters of those coordinators were, as part of their role, involved with provision for special educational needs.

During the introduction of the National Curriculum there were, despite HMI's support for the role of special educational needs coordinator, reports that special needs posts were being cut and that in primary schools these were being replaced by coordinators for National Curriculum subjects (Coopers and Lybrand Deloitte 1991, Fletcher-Campbell 1993). The cutting of special educational needs posts (coordinators/learning support) was reported to have occurred in 15 per cent of local education authorities (House of Commons 1993). To some extent what may have been happening was not a loss of posts but a redefining and narrowing of the subject focus in broadly oriented coordinator roles.

The recommendations in the Code of Practice can be seen as an attempt to develop the special needs focus in coordinator posts. Making the Code work will be dependent to a large extent on developing the special needs coordinator as an effective role. The demands and possibilities of this coordinator, as outlined in the Code, are extensive (see Chapter 8). There is a mismatch between the guidelines in the Code and the situation in schools. A national survey of special needs provision in mainstream primary schools found that the large majority of the schools (94 per cent) had a named teacher with responsibility for children with special needs in the school (Lewis 1995a). However, the vast majority of special needs coordinators were also class teachers and many (61 per cent) had additional responsibilities as well as special needs. Two-thirds of the special needs coordinators had no time, or less than one hour a week, to carry out development and coordination of special needs provision. Only 8 per cent had five hours a week or more to devote to special needs coordinator duties. This suggests that most of the teachers currently acting as special needs co-ordinators will find it difficult to fulfil the range of demands embodied in the Code. If this is so then it threatens the effec-tiveness of a switch in emphasis from statemented to non-statemented provision.

The changing infrastructure of special needs provision

What structures are in place to support the coordinator and other mainstream staff in relation to children with special educational needs? This question is answered here in relation to two aspects of support: training about special needs and the availability, at Local Education Authority level, of expertise about special needs.

Training in special educational needs

Until recently the predominant pattern of special needs provision for mainstream primary schools was of part-time teachers carry-ing out withdrawal group work, supported by advice from the Local Education Authority's peripatetic special needs services. Local Education Authority special needs training and external secondments were heavily directed towards members of those teams. While this developed the skills of the specialist teams it neglected the development of special educational needs expertise in mainstream schools. The 1987 Primary Staffing Survey (DES 1987a) found that 90 per cent of the full-time primary teachers in England with 'special educational needs leadership respons-ibility' had no qualifications in special educational needs.

Alongside a shift towards an emphasis on all teachers as having responsibilities for children with special educational needs has come a broadening of the groups at whom special educational needs INSET has been directed. There was an injection of funding through Grant 12 of the 1993–4 GEST programme in training for teachers of children with special needs. Over 30 per cent (£2.3 million) of this expenditure was used for training special needs coordinators in mainstream schools. Over 5,700 teachers were involved in this programme but little is known about the quality, range or coherence of this training. While low-level training is to be welcomed in providing awareness of special needs issues this training needs to be part of a wider structure of available curricular expertise and resources. Some local education authorities have made arrangements with higher education institutions through which local authority in-service training is validated and can contribute to modular programmes leading to a pyramid of diplomas, advanced certificates, higher and research degrees.

Local Education Authority special needs support

The Code of Practice states that (at stage 3) the special needs coordinator should call in an appropriate specialist from a support service when assessing the child's needs. This person 'will be qualified and experienced in the particular area of the child's special educational needs' (para. 2.104). Are local education authorities equipped to provide such expertise? Local authorities have been reluctant to delegate the funding of learning support services (Garner et al. 1991, Audit Commission 1994). However, the shifting local authority role from provider to monitor of special needs provision, combined with the effects of the local management of schools, is leading to a reduction in the pool of special needs expertise centralised in the local authorities.

Emphasis on partnership with parents

Another shift has been formal recognition of the importance of partnerships between schools and the parents of children with special needs. Comparisons between draft and final versions of the Code of Practice illustrate the increased prominence given to providing information to, consulting with, and obtaining evidence from, the child's parents.

The Code reinstates the role of the Named Person, an idea put forward in the Warnock Report (DES 1978b) but not taken up previously. The Named Person is someone, preferably independent of the Local Education Authority, who can give the parent information and advice about their child's special needs. The Code states that if the Local Education Authority does make a statement then the Authority must write to the parents confirming the identity of the Named Person (para. 3.11). Similarly, the DFE's guide to parents about special needs reiterates this point and also includes names and addresses of appropriate organisations. Inevitably, because of the types of groups represented by, or in, voluntary organisations, the list is biased towards physical disabilities, sensory impairments and severe learning difficulties. Mainstream schools will have to find ways of working effectively with a variety of voluntary and charitable groups in the special needs field. This will parallel what is already happening in health and social services.

There are relatively few parent groups oriented specifically to children with mild or moderate learning difficulties or emotional and behavioural problems. Yet proportionately, these are the largest special needs groups. It may be difficult for schools and local education authorities to balance those children's needs against the interests of minority, but strongly represented, special needs groups.

Greater accountability concerning mainstream special needs provision

The Audit Commission found that:

> LEAs [local education authorities (surveyed in 1993)] did not have effective systems in place to hold schools to account for their work with pupils with special needs. Most LEAs did not attend annual reviews of pupils with statements and also had no other means of measuring the performance of schools with all pupils with special educational needs.
>
> (Audit Commission 1994: 10)

All schools are being made more accountable for their special needs provision. One way in which this is happening is by requiring schools to publish their special needs policies. Regulations have detailed the information that schools must provide (DFE 1994c). This includes: the name of the person in the school with day-to-day responsibility for special needs, the basis for allocating special needs resources, the basis for evaluating the curriculum for children with special needs, parental complaints procedures and the use made of external agencies/groups.

Governors have an important role, under the Code, for making sure that this information is provided. However, their responsibilities for special needs provision extend beyond this. They must also: consult, where necessary or desirable in order to coordinate special needs provision, with the Local Education Authority, the Funding Agency for Schools, and the governing bodies of other schools; ensure (given certain provisos) that children with special needs join in activities with other children; and report annually to parents about special needs policies. These duties are in addition to the complex responsibilities which they have in relation to the making of disapplications and temporary exceptions from the National Curriculum. Given these responsibilities it will be important that all mainstream schools have at least one governor (in larger, or a cluster of, schools a group of governors) with a special needs remit. One-third of primary schools surveyed recently had no such governor (Lewis 1995a). Unfortunately there is little systematic evidence about which governors take on a special needs role or the impact that such governors have on a school's special needs policy.

A tightening of the legal framework of special needs provision

The concomitant of mainstream schools becoming more accountable for their special needs policies is the increasingly legalistic framework growing up around the provision of services for children with special needs. If parents are dissatisfied with the special needs provision received by their child then they can complain to the school, to the Local Education Authority, to the Secretary of State, to a regional special needs tribunal, to the ombudsman and, ultimately, to the European Court.

The 1993 Education Act introduced the regional special needs tribunals. This was, at least in part, to deal with the increasing number of appeals to the Secretary of State. There were 26,000 statements issued in England in 1991. Although the number of appeals has been increasing it is still a very small proportion of the total number of statements issued each year. Appeals against either the issuing (or not) of a statement or the content of a statement increased steadily between 1984 (just after the 1981 Act took effect) and 1991. In approximately two-thirds of these cases the appeal result supported the Local Education Authority (Audit Commission/HMI 1992).

Alongside this increase was a parallel rise in complaints made about special needs provision to the ombudsman. Recourse to the ombudsman is increasing although this too is still a very small proportion of all cases in which statements are issued. In the large majority of instances the ombudsman found no support for a claim of maladministration by the Local Education Authority. These levels of complaints about special needs provision are reflected in the projection that the special needs regional tribunals are expected to deal with 700–1,000 cases in the first year of operation.

In a climate of legal action as a way of obtaining provision, the confident, the articulate, those with time, knowledge, energy and perhaps money to devote to pursuing a case will in the end obtain an unbalanced share of scarce resources. There is a danger that children with less confident, less interested, less well-informed or less articulate parents will not get the resources they need. These concerns have been supported by reports about the 235 cases registered, between September 1994 and January 1995, for special needs tribunals (Pyke 1995). More than half these cases had been filed on behalf of children with dyslexia. Parents of these children have a right, and an understandable concern, to obtain the best provision for their children. Good working relations between schools, Local Education Authorities, the Named Person, pressure and voluntary groups will be important if demands are to be realistic and appropriate for the child. In addition, some checks are needed in the system if more numerous, but less vigorous, special needs groups are to be fairly represented and resourced through such procedures.

The confrontational approach undermines an assumption that teachers will do their best for the pupils they teach. Mutual trust and respect between parents and professionals is damaged by an expectation of the need to resort to legal measures. Recourse to legal action implies that schools are being obstinate about not providing for special needs, yet many schools do not have the resources to provide for children with special needs as the teachers and parents would wish. Expectations about special needs provision have escalated, probably to hopelessly unrealistic levels when set against schools' and Local Education Authorities' resources. This can only be detrimental to partnership between parents and teachers.

CONCLUSION

The National Curriculum is a curriculum for all children and this book is about the strategies which teachers might use to give all children access to that curriculum. Many of the examples given relate to the core subjects but the strategies could be applied across all curricular areas. Despite the positive stance of this introduction, there are some worrying aspects of the National Curriculum and these are discussed in the relevant chapters. The following two chapters focus on the range of the curriculum for children with difficulties in learning. This is discussed first as a general issue (Chapter 2) and then in relation to implications for practice (Chapter 3).

Chapter 2

Safeguarding a broad curriculum

At the heart of the 1988 Education Reform Act lies a contradiction. Sections 1 and 2 of the Act reflect contrasting approaches to aims and content in education. Section 1 is broad, referring to the need for a curriculum which promotes 'spiritual, moral, cultural, mental and physical development' and prepares pupils for the 'opportunities, responsibilities and experiences of adult life'. By contrast, Section 2 of the Act discusses the planned outlines of work in the discrete foundation subjects (plus religious education). Section 2 is, overwhelmingly, addressing only part of the aims given in Section 1; the broader aims are not met by the statutory programmes of study.

There have been attempts to bridge this gap in two ways. First, it has been stated that subject-specific programmes of study, attainment targets and assessment arrangements do not constitute the whole curriculum (National Curriculum Council 1989b, SCAA 1994a). A child's whole curriculum should be wider than these in order to meet the aims of Section 1 of the Education Reform Act. The National Curriculum Council's Curriculum Guidance 3 was categorical about this: 'The National Curriculum alone will not provide the necessary breadth' (National Curriculum Council 1990a: 1). This position was the outcome of a hard-won battle. Politically, the Whole Curriculum Committee was unpopular: 'The [National Curriculum] Council was told [by civil servants] that its job was to deliver the ten national curriculum subjects; everything else could be dealt with once the original brief was achieved' (Graham 1993a: 20). Duncan Graham, Chairman and Chief Executive of the National Curriculum Council (1988–91) reviewing the introduction of the National Curriculum concluded: 'A real success has been the preservation and enhancement of the whole curriculum ... A right wing attempt to restrict it [the National Curriculum] to statutory provision was thwarted – the National Curriculum Council's finest hour?' (Graham 1993b: 7).

The need for schools to have greater flexibility and so go beyond the National Curriculum was recognised in the revised (i.e. 1995) National Curriculum documentation. This took up the suggestion made in Ron Dearing's final report that the equivalent of one day a week should be released 'for schools to use at their own discretion' (SCAA 1994b: 5). This suggestion was not as radical as at first appeared given that originally the National Curriculum was not intended to be the whole curriculum. However, it was an interesting statement of support for the National Curriculum Council's earlier position and contrasted with the reported pressures from civil servants and ministers. In practice, schools had tended to treat the National Curriculum as the whole curriculum in order to get through all the content that seemed to be required. This led some headteachers to talk and write of 'Sod the National Curriculum' weeks in which there were occasional, jubilant weeks of non-National Curriculum activities:

> With increasing despondency I watched interesting elements of school life being marginalised as we tried to shoehorn the requirements of the National Curriculum into the school day ... The SNC [Sod the National Curriculum] week is planned to give children experiences that they will remember for a lifetime ... Horizons will be lifted for all of us. We will have excitement, pleasure and fun – three activities which fail to be mentioned in the many volumes of National Curriculum documents.
>
> (Sullivan 1993: 5)

Ron Dearing's proposal was a restatement of the original position, sharpened by (a) placing a quantity on non-National Curriculum time and (b) facilitating a decrease in content. This made more realistic the possibility of exploiting non-National Curriculum time.

Second, cross-curricular elements have been posited as ways of developing non-subject-specific material. Cross-curricular elements encompass: dimensions (for example, equal opportunities) which are 'concerned with the intentional promotion of personal and social development through the curriculum as a whole' (National Curriculum Council 1989b: para. 9); skills (referred to as 'competencies' in the early National Curriculum documentation), such as numeracy and personal skills, which are developed through several different aspects of the curriculum; and themes (for example, citizenship, environmental education) which are essential parts of the whole curriculum but which may straddle one or more of the foundation subjects. For example, elements of citizenship feature in geography and history programmes of study. Themes could also go beyond the basic curriculum of the foundation subjects and religious education. To continue the example of citizenship, this might reasonably include the development of a caring attitude towards others. There has been considerable variation in which topics have been identified as themes in successive National Curriculum documents. Citizenship, which at first did not appear, became one of the five 'pre-eminent' themes (National Curriculum Council 1990a). The revised (i.e. 1995) National Curriculum makes relatively little reference to cross-curricular elements. Although the cross-curricular elements have been regarded as important ways of presenting National Curriculum material in many special schools, they seem to have been relatively neglected in mainstream schools (Lewis and Halpin 1994, Costley 1994, Webb 1993).

POSSIBLE LIMITATIONS TO A BROAD CURRICULUM FOR CHILDREN WITH DIFFICULTIES IN LEARNING

There are three identifiable forces which are likely to operate to diminish the curricular breadth of the whole curriculum as described in the Education Reform Act. These three forces are: (a) uncertainties about the foci of entitlement, (b) differences between the status of subjects because of end of key stage assessments and (c) available curriculum time. The first two of these forces are likely to apply more sharply to children with learning difficulties than to other pupils, the third will apply to all children.

An entitlement to what?

There are two aspects to this question. First, what specific aspects of the curriculum are covered by statute and so, by law, the subject of entitlement? Second, what is more broadly interpreted as a child's educational entitlement?

The first of these questions was answered by the National

Curriculum Council: 'The National Curriculum (which is statutory) is non-negotiable as a framework for every school and as an entitlement for all pupils' (National Curriculum Council 1989c: 2.5). This raises in turn the question of what is the statutory National Curriculum? Subject-specific programmes of study, attainment targets, level descriptions and assessment arrangements are statutory; much cross-curricular work and all work outside the non-'basic curriculum' are only advisory. The National Curriculum Council acknowledged the ambiguous position of the cross-curricular themes: 'Where these themes are embedded in the National Curriculum programmes of study they are statutory' (National Curriculum Council 1989b: para. 16). This position was reiterated more recently:

> Cross-curricular themes have never been statutory but there is no reason why schools should not introduce them through the statutory curriculum.
>
> (Unnamed spokesman for the Schools Curriculum and Assessment Authority, quoted in Todd 1994)

Thus cross-curricular elements are only statutory where they are included in statutory subject Orders.

In answer to the second of the earlier questions about the focus of educational entitlement, the National Curriculum Council recognised that 'Other aspects [i.e. not encompassed by subject Orders], while not statutory, are clearly required if schools are to provide an education which promotes the aims defined in section 1 of the Education Reform Act' (National Curriculum Council 1989b: para. 16).

Teachers of children who have difficulties in learning often emphasise the importance of developing the children's self-confidence, communication skills and enthusiasm for learning. These teachers may feel that attaining specific subject targets is comparatively unimportant for those children. This creates a potential dilemma. For example, one child may need speech therapy in order to communicate more effectively with others, another child may need small-group therapy to help to overcome emotional difficulties and so collaborate with classmates. In both these examples, the prior need will militate against a broad and balanced curriculum, at least in the short term. Yet without specific help the child may be hampered from benefiting from the broader curriculum. Teachers are likely to decide that the broader educational entitlement should take precedence over the narrower curricular entitlement. It is significant that in the Code of Practice (DFE 1994a) the individual education plan for a child with special educational needs is not confined to National Curriculum requirements.

Assessment tests and tasks: Another threat to breadth?

End of key stage assessments were referred to as standard assessment tasks (SATs) during the introductory period of the National Curriculum. This term has subsequently been used less often (partly due to the use of SAT in the American context to refer to scholastic aptitude test) and has been largely replaced by the phrase 'end of key stage tests and tasks'. 'End of key stage tests and tasks' is used here to cover both phrases. The early development of these tests and tasks focused on the core subjects of English, mathematics and science. However, the letters from the DES to chairs of working groups indicated that, initially, it was intended that all foundation subjects should be assessed, in part, through nationally prescribed tests. This planned breadth of end of key stage tests and tasks has since been reduced considerably (see Chapter 10).

If headteachers and teachers feel under pressure to be seen to have good results on reported assessments then children with difficulties in learning may come to be regarded as the children who will 'pull down' a school's results. As a consequence there may be a temptation to give those children more work on reported areas and less work on other aspects. In wider educational terms this would clearly be undesirable. It may also be counterproductive since, as discussed in Chapter 3, broad integrated work may well provide the basis for learning to apply and to generalise skills and knowledge, and to maximise children's motivation, thereby indirectly leading to improved attainments. The impact of the publication of test results will differ across key stages 1 and 2 as it has been decided that end of key stage 1 results will not be published but those at the end of key stage 2 will be. The effect of this may be to defer from age 6–7 to age 9–10 attempts to move children from mainstream into special schools. Before considering how schools might meet the demands for breadth in curriculum content, it is worth reviewing the advice concerning time allocations in specific foundation subjects. This affects the curricula for all children, including those with difficulties in learning.

Time allocations for foundation subjects in the National Curriculum

The consultation document on the National Curriculum (DES 1987b) tried to map possible timetable allocations for foundation subjects at secondary school level but did not do this for primary schools. It stated only that, 'The *majority of curriculum time* at primary level should be devoted to the core subjects' (para. 14; my emphasis). In the Education Reform Act the ten subjects in the basic curriculum have not been given time allocations, either individually or grouped, within a school's timetable. The 1988 Education Act specifically excluded this and also prevented Orders from being made to bring in such time allocations. However, schools do have to spend a 'reasonable time' on foundation subjects so that children carry out 'worthwhile work' (DES 1989a). Ron Dearing's review (SCAA 1994a, 1994b) suggested that 80 per cent of the teaching week should be spent on work related to the National Curriculum. The conclusion from a series of regional conferences on possible revisions to the National Curriculum in relation to children with special needs was that a notional target figure of 70 per cent of time for the National Curriculum was appropriate (National Curriculum Council 1993a). Some headteachers in special schools have argued that this is too high for pupils in their schools and that a reasonable figure there would be 30 per cent (Lewis and Halpin 1994). So teachers concerned about children with special educational needs may want to find ways of releasing more non-National Curriculum time.

Individual draft proposals for each of the foundation subjects (DFE 1995) make no reference to specific subject time allocations. The vagueness, or flexibility, about time allocations for individual subjects leaves headteachers and teachers with considerable freedom concerning how they plan the curriculum. Although there have been recommendations about notional time allocations for individual subjects (generally in the supplementary guidance to the chairs of working parties), these are not part of the legal requirements of the National Curriculum. Time allocations (as a percentage of the teaching week) for subjects at key stages 1 and 2 have been suggested (See Table 2.1).

Table 2.1 Suggested time allocations for subjects at key stages 1 and 2

Subject	Time allocation
• English	20 per cent
• Mathematics	20 per cent
• Science and technology*	12.5 per cent
• History	7.5–10 per cent
• Geography	7.5–10 per cent
• Art	[6–7.5 per cent]
• Music	[5 per cent]
• PE	(5 per cent)
• Religious education	(5 per cent)

Source: Taken from *Education*, 3 April 1992.
Notes: Working group figures, based on practice, are shown in square brackets.
Notional figures are shown in parentheses.
* Technology was subsequently redesignated design and technology, plus
information technology (SCAA 1994a).

Alert readers will have noticed that the figures in Table 2.1
(excluding religious education) add up to 83.5–90 per cent so
(assuming no double counting) they will have to be reduced
further to bring them into line with Ron Dearing's (SCAA 1994b)
proposal that the National Curriculum occupy 80 per cent of
curriculum time.

On the basis of these figures, about 70 per cent of the teaching
week is taken up by the core subjects, plus technology, history and
geography. This leaves 10 per cent of the teaching week for music,
art and PE, while religious education, all cross-curricular themes
(where these are taught separately from foundation subjects) and
any non-National Curriculum work will fill the remaining 20 per
cent of the week. Areas such as art and PE are notoriously time
consuming in primary, especially infant, schools. A 30-minute
swimming period, for example, could easily occupy 90 minutes if
the time required for transporting children to and from an off-site
pool and for changing is taken into account. This also illustrates
the difficulties in defining time spent on specific curricular areas
at primary level. Most teachers take advantage of opportunities
such as a bus journey to the swimming baths to develop children's
observations of the area, to practise various rhymes or singing
games or to talk with individual children.

The issue of time allocation was highlighted in HMI's (DES
1989c) first report on the implementation of the National Curriculum in primary schools. HMI found that 70 per cent of teaching

time for children in year 1 was being spent on the core subjects although few classes taught the core subjects entirely separately. HMI concluded that 'Many schools are not well prepared to meet the reasonable time requirements, especially in areas such as technology, history or geography' (DES 1989c: para. 48). The emphasis on core subjects in the schools surveyed in summer 1989 may reflect the fact that the first National Curriculum subject documents to be published focused on these subjects. These documents were followed by the technology interim report in June 1989, by the history working party report in August 1989 and by other subject reports later. Even so, as history, geography, technology, and presumably PE, art and music were receiving insufficient time, it is unsurprising that activities outside the National Curriculum were not being developed.

The explicit recognition for some non-National Curriculum time (SCAA 1994a, 1994b) reflects this position. All subjects, including the core, have been reduced in content in the revised National Curriculum. Schools may still find it difficult to provide the breadth of curriculum specified. Jim Campbell and Hilary Emery (1994), in a review of time spent teaching English and Mathematics in primary schools, have shown that there is a very strong tendency for about 50 per cent of time to be spent on these two subject areas (i.e. in total). That tendency has applied to primary schools in England over the last twenty years, including in the period since the introduction of the National Curriculum. Interestingly, schools for primary age children in many cultural, historical and political contexts have shown this same propensity for about half the teaching time to be spent on language and mathematics. Thus to attempt to change this (as the National Curriculum set out to do) runs counter to very deep-seated tendencies in primary education. The subjects that have been squeezed out in the primary school curriculum, compared with National Curriculum target times, have been history, geography and religious education (Campbell and Emery 1994).

RESPONDING TO PRESSURES OF TIME

How can more time be made available for non-National Curriculum work?

The school day is short. One study of ILEA junior schools (Mortimore *et al.* 1988) found that the average teaching time in a day (i.e. excluding playtimes, dinner times, assembly, etc.) was approximately five hours. Even within this 'teaching day', time available for learning is curtailed. Barbara Tizard and her team (1988) found that non-work activities within the infant classroom (such as wandering about, tidying up, going to the lavatories and registration) took up 17 per cent of children's time in the school day. A group of researchers reviewing the impact of the National Curriculum at key stage 2 concluded that the introduction of the National Curriculum did not appear to have had an effect overall on the amount of time in which children were engaged with educational activities (Sammons *et al.* 1994). No matter how efficiently classroom time is organised there will always be some time spent on essential and legitimate non-work activities.

There are two ways of increasing learning time in schools: to 'add time' and to use available time more effectively. In addition, in the context of the National Curriculum, there are various ways, such as 'double-counting' subject time, to increase time available for non-National Curriculum work.

Increasing the time available for teaching/learning

The Inner London Education Authority's junior school study (Mortimore *et al.* 1988) showed the diversity in time in school between different schools. Some children had a school day which was regularly 40 minutes longer than that of other children. Over several school years such a difference would accumulate into a substantial difference in total time in school. A minimum teaching week (i.e. total lesson time) of 21 hours for reception to year 2 or 23.5 hours for years 3–6 has been recommended (DFE 1994d).

Schools with a short day could consider ways of extending the day, perhaps by being more flexible about when children come into school. Do children have to wait outside (possibly in the cold) or, if a teacher is present, can they go into the classroom and start on activities? Many schools now have a much more flexible start to the school day in order to capitalise on children's enthusiasm for learning. The introduction of different patterns to the school day (the 'continental' day) or term (a four-term, rather than a three-term school year) may also use learning time better than more traditional patterns. A special school headteacher told me that one result of the implementation of the National Curriculum in his school had been to start school half an hour earlier each morning (at 9.00 not 9.30) and to cut out the mid-afternoon break. The commonality of the National Curriculum in special and mainstream schools had led him and his staff to question whether a comparatively late start was really necessary. The mid-afternoon break was reconsidered and seen as a legacy from the days when the special school pupils had been thought to need a brief sleep mid-afternoon. The changes to the school day increased teaching time by 50 minutes every day. This adds up to over four hours a week and, if we take a timetabled teaching day as approximately five hours and a school year as 40 weeks, this is roughly an (astonishing) extra 33 teaching days over a school year. Primary teachers are, as discussed in Chapter 1, typically working a 50-hour week. Much of this time is spent on work away from the children. It would be unreasonable and probably counter-productive to try to increase teachers' work time on top of this notional 50 hours. So any increase in the length of the teaching day should go alongside strategies to reduce work outside the classroom.

Ways of creating additional teaching/learning time also include being more flexible about mid-morning, mid-afternoon and lunch-time breaks. There may be ways of allowing children to carry on working over these times and taking shorter breaks if they choose to do so. This might entail having a rota of supervisors in the playground over, say, 30 minutes, and doubling up class super-vision for short periods. Alternatively, breaks could be used more constructively, not just for children to 'let off steam' but as a time during which children play at various number or language games in a semi-structured way. In one London school in which I taught, the head regularly used 'wet' playtimes as a period when she supervised the whole school and taught the children traditional London street rhymes and singing games. By the time the children left the school they had a large store of these which they shared with friends from other schools, taught to (or reminded) parents and older relatives, and spontaneously sang and played in the playground and streets.

Simple marking out of the playground in a variety of ways (for example, hopscotch, overlapping circles, dartboard patterns) can foster better use of this facility. Interestingly, the New Zealand Government has produced a comprehensive handbook of play-ground ideas, which is distributed to all primary school teachers. This is an idea which could be copied in Britain and would perhaps be received more enthusiastically than some of the

National Curriculum documents. Similarly, if the playground is turned into a more interesting environment then it can become a rich source for learning. Some schools have made imaginative conversions of their playgrounds from bald asphalt to multi-sensory wildlife environments in which different types of garden are developed in different areas of the playground. In such a school much environmental education can take place during playtimes. Peter Blatchford (1989) describes a wonderful example of such a school in Berkshire. I know also of schools in 'deprived' inner city areas in which similar conversions have been made, sometimes in the face of opponents who have feared that the attractive school environment would be rapidly vandalised. However, these fears have proved unjustified.

Using classroom learning time more effectively

A second way of making more time for learning is by using timetabled learning time more effectively; for example, by keeping routine administrative tasks to a minimum. The register could be completed by noting informally which children are present/ absent rather than making all children stop their activities to listen to the register. Similarly, if children are tuned into regular routines (such as knowing the time at which assembly takes place), they will get into the habit of stopping activities just before this time. Judicious use of class, group and individual work in which pupil grouping is matched appropriately to task demands is increasingly recognised as central to making the most of learning time (Alexander *et al.* 1992). If children are intended to work as a group then it is relevant and helpful to seat children in groups. If children are participating in a teacher-led class activity then sitting in small groups may be distracting and inappropriate. Similarly, classroom organisation and the organisation of resources should fit together. Rea Reason (1993) notes that collaborative group work can enhance children's learning as well as freeing the teacher to work in greater depth for sustained periods with individuals. These and other aspects of using classroom learning time effectively are discussed in Chapters 7 and 8.

One of the biggest challenges for the teacher of a child who has difficulties in school-based learning is to sustain the child's confidence and enthusiasm in learning. The greatest disincentive in learning anything is to experience repeated failure. Even adults, who should be relatively confident and mature, tend to react to failure by wanting to avoid the activity which prompted the failure. As a worker involved in an adult literacy scheme, I met many adults who had gone to great lengths to hide their inabilities to read or write competently, rather than try again to learn these skills. One woman was an Avon cosmetics representative who managed the whole process of taking and sending in orders by pointing to pictures and copying numbers from one form to another. When she explained to me how she sent in and then checked the orders it was clear that she had developed elements which worked and avoided any 'reading'. It was her inability to read stories to her daughter which had prompted her long-delayed, and ultimately successful, attempt at learning to read. Similarly, one man who had minimal reading skills ran a large and successful business. He said that no one at his business knew of his poor reading because he dictated everything to his secretary and she read important incoming mail onto a dicta-phone machine.

Many teachers can recount the variety of minor ways in which some children will try to avoid a particular task. Sometimes this avoidance stems from failure and fear of failing again. Sharpening pencils, cleaning out the hamster's cage, sorting the book area, taking a note round to other classes or dinner numbers to the secretary, all seem to be well-tried ploys. Few children go to the lengths of one child I knew (a 9-year-old boy) who ate the school goldfish rather than attempt, yet again, an activity which he found difficult. Such behaviour prompts questions about the curriculum and the actions of the teacher as well as of the child.

Children with learning difficulties may often try to avoid 'work' in schools. Diana Moses (1982), in an interesting study of junior school classes, found that although teachers spent more time with 'slow learners' than they did with 'average' children, the 'slow learners' were engaged in work or 'partial work' for just over half the time whereas 'average' children worked for nearly 70 per cent of the time. A range of research has shown that 'time on task' is closely correlated with attainment and, although one should be wary of making simplistic judgements about time on task (for example, children staring vacantly into space may be thinking through a problem), it seems that a crucial issue for class teachers is how to find ways of maximising learning time and encouraging children with learning difficulties to carry on with learning activities.

Defining time allocations in the National Curriculum

In the context of the National Curriculum there may be scope for teaching material outside the foundation subjects by a 'double-counting' of the time spent teaching particular foundation subjects. For example, a discussion about a plant growing in the classroom could fulfil several parts of different programmes of study (for example, English, science, geography and mathematics). Circular 6 (National Curriculum Council 1989b) makes explicit reference to 'sharing attainment targets' (para. 12) so that, for example, oracy is developed across subject areas. The paragraph is written from the perspective of a secondary school ('The English teacher . . . the mathematics teacher') but in the primary context it can be seen as a recognition that some aspects of programmes of study will be developed through several 'subjects'. Revisions to the National Curriculum have eliminated some duplication between subjects and so curtailed scope for double counting where the same activity might be counted twice, rather than where different aspects of one task might reasonably count under two subjects.

CONCLUSION

At the start of this chapter I quoted the National Curriculum Council's (1990a) Curriculum Guidance 3 which stated that the basic curriculum (i.e. the National Curriculum plus religious education) should not be the whole curriculum. It is important to hold on to this idea if curricula in schools are to be broadened, not narrowed, through the implementation of the National Curriculum. Charles Handy, an economist and management consultant, uses the metaphor of a doughnut to describe the relationship, in various contexts, of core areas to periphery. He uses the idea of an inverted (American) doughnut – that is one with a solid centre surrounded by space – to convey the concept of balance between the essential and the potential (Handy 1994). The core contains what has to be done. In the educational context we could see this as the National Curriculum and religious education. The core is not the whole. The periphery contains areas which provide opportunities for individual development and to 'go beyond the bounds of duty' (Handy 1994: 66). He suggests that the quality of a life, a job, an organisation, a relationship or a curriculum, lies not in the core alone but in the balance between core and periphery. Chapter 3 considers some practical implications of working towards a curriculum which has breadth in several ways or, in Charles Handy's terms, a balance between core and periphery.

Chapter 3

Planning for a broad curriculum

Worries about the National Curriculum narrowing learning opportunities, especially for children with difficulties in learning, have
prompted teachers to look imaginatively at ways of countering
such possible narrowing. Two aspects of curricular breadth will be
considered here: broad frameworks for the planning of teaching/
learning, and strategies to promote later, as well as initial, stages
of learning. Topic-based approaches will be discussed as a specific
way of promoting various stages of learning.

FRAMEWORKS FOR PLANNING TEACHING

There have been three frameworks put forward as ways of
planning for a broad curriculum within the demands of the
National Curriculum and the 1994 Code of Practice. These frameworks apply to whole class planning, including work with children
who find learning difficult.

Starting from National Curriculum subjects and cross-curricular themes

The most conventional solution is to list the foundation subjects,
religious education and cross-curricular themes and to plan work
to cover all these areas. This is probably the most straightforward
way through which to show that a school is teaching the National
Curriculum. The work may be taught within subject blocks or
utilising topic work. This approach is embodied in material
produced by Northamptonshire (NIAS 1992) in which coloured
tickets identifying individual attainment targets are to be de-
tached from the folder and physically spread out to produce a

large 'curriculum map' ('PoS plus'). Teachers are encouraged 'to make decisions on the subject emphasis for those areas which you have decided will fit together' (NIAS 1992: 13).

Topic work can be used narrowly (i.e. single subject-based) or, more creatively and complexly, as subject-linked. The single subject-based approach might involve using a topic like 'transport' to teach part of the history curriculum, perhaps adding elements from art programmes of study. The subject-linked approach might take the same topic (transport in this example) and through this teach a variety of aspects of different programmes of study, for example, mathematics (for example, calculations involving timetables), geography (for example, analyses of the influence of the landscape on transport patterns), design and technology (for example, development of the principles involved in designing a vehicle for off-road use in deserts), English and music (for example, reading, writing and evaluating poetry with a strong rhythmic base reflecting different forms of transport), science (for example, understanding of gravitational forces) and history (for example, knowledge of the development of road transport). Duncan Graham was describing a subject-linked approach to topic work when he wrote:

> The [National Curriculum] content need not be delivered in subject form – 'throwing all the attainment targets on the floor' and reassembling them could, at a stroke, reduce overlap, volume and pressure. It could also put some excitement back.
>
> (Graham 1993b: 7)

Materials produced by Wiltshire Advisory Services (1992) reflect a modified version of this approach. Through these materials teachers are encouraged to plan some teaching around themes. An early stage in such an approach to curriculum planning is to brainstorm ideas relating to the theme ('growth' is given as an example). The next stage is to refine the focus and to select a few areas identified through the 'brainstorming' exercise. A planning web and a check against National Curriculum attainment targets, and cross-curricular themes and skills follow from this.

It has been reported that primary schools have been reluctant to abandon well-established patterns of curriculum organisation and have continued to use topic work as the main means for organising and teaching the curriculum (National Curriculum Council 1993b). Similar findings have been reported elsewhere

(Webb 1993). Interestingly, within this continuing use of topics, there has been increasing use of subject-focused topics, usually science, history or geography. What does not seem to have been happening is the sort of highly integrated approach to topic work described by Duncan Graham. One factor may have been the conclusions of a report, commissioned by the Secretary of State, on curriculum organisation and classroom practice in primary schools. This report was sceptical about the value of unfocused topic work and concluded 'When topic work focuses on a clearly defined and limited number of attainment targets it, too, can make an important contribution to the development of pupil learning' (Alexander *et al.* 1992: 35).

There is comparatively little systematic evidence about the implementation of the National Curriculum in special schools. However, there are indications that, in contrast to the mainstream sector, special schools working with primary age children with learning difficulties have retained a multi-focused approach to topic work (Lewis and Halpin 1994). This has created an interesting situation in which very different approaches to teaching the National Curriculum to children with learning difficulties can be identified. This provides a potentially rich source of evidence about the diversity of effective ways through which to teach the National Curriculum.

Motivational value of topic-based work

In Chapter 2, issues to do with time spent learning and ways of maximising this were discussed. One way of utilising children's motivation for learning and of building on this is to encourage children to develop their own interests through topic- or project-based learning. Topic work, even when teacher-initiated, reflects a belief that children learn more effectively if subject-centred material is taught in a broader way, although as noted earlier individual topics may contain a bias towards a certain subject area.

The extent to which a topic approach to developing learning is motivating for children may depend on how the topic is chosen. Ways of introducing topics range from wholly child-centred to more strongly teacher-initiated. At the child-centred end are situations in which learning develops naturally from a child's firsthand experiences (as when a child playing with junk modelling materials makes a model of a house and this is then developed with teacher guidance into an exploration of the properties of materials, stories about the people who live in the house, estimates of wallpaper to cover it, etc.). This approach requires much careful teacher guidance of children and direct teaching when the need for this is apparent. Its great strength is that it starts with the child's interests but difficulty arises in ensuring progression, balance and breadth in learning.

At the teacher-initiated end of the continuum are topics which are introduced by the teacher and which depend on his or her skill to make them link with the child's experiences. In teacher-initiated topic work, the topics are often planned through the school as a whole with particular topics (usually history, geography, science, design and technology) being allocated to specific years and terms. The last terms in years 2 and 6 may be left 'open' for work associated with end of key stage assessment tests and tasks. The selection of the topics reflects a search for a way of encompassing work which is required in at least several of the foundation subjects without timetabling rigid slots for each of the ten subjects in the basic curriculum. Children with learning difficulties should be included in the class topic and Chapter 6 includes examples of how work in two topics could be developed concurrently by children of different attainments. An advantage of such planning of a series of topics is that it tries to ensure, at least at the planning stage, systematic coverage of National Curriculum programmes of study. A disadvantage is that it diminishes teachers' scope for developing topics spontaneously as they arise from children's interests.

Starting from cross-curricular elements

A second approach to planning coverage of the National Curriculum is to start with the cross-curricular elements, rather than subject-based documentation, and to plan the curriculum around the cross-curricular elements. This has intuitive appeal for many primary school teachers. In this approach a school might begin by listing cross-curricular dimensions, leading to a policy statement of school principles in relation to issues such as equal opportunities. Then the school might look at cross-curricular themes (not only the National Curriculum Council's 'pre-eminent' five) and map how these will be taught across and within classes. Next, cross-curricular skills are reviewed to check that these are being developed with continuity and progression. These three sets of cross-curricular elements lead to reference to subject documentation. Thus, at the planning stage, the processes of learning and, in particular, the development of personal and social skills come before subject-centred knowledge. This approach has been used successfully in some special schools, for example, those for children with severe learning difficulties. For these pupils subject-centred learning has involved only the first few levels of relevant attainment targets. It is more difficult (although possible) to translate the approach into contexts in which children will be acquiring a wide range of subject-specific knowledge, concepts and skills.

Starting from areas of learning and experience

A third way of planning for curricular breadth is to take an alternative framework from that of the National Curriculum. One such framework is that provided by HMI (DES 1985) in which nine areas of learning and experience were outlined. These were:

- Aesthetic and creative
- Human and social
- Linguistic and literary
- Mathematical
- Moral

- Physical
- Scientific
- Spiritual
- Technological

These have been widely quoted and some authorities, notably Leicestershire in their key stages materials (Leicestershire Local Education Authority 1989), developed ways of cross-referencing attainment targets with these areas of learning and experience. The appeal of this approach is that it retains an overall breadth (explicitly including human, social, spiritual and moral aspects of education) as well as approaching subject-based work from a wide disciplinary base (for example, aesthetic, scientific and physical areas). The validity of these areas has been debated but they have much in common with theoretical models such as the forms of knowledge proposed by Paul Hirst (1974).

CURRICULAR BREADTH: PLANNING FOR VARIOUS STAGES OF LEARNING AND TEACHING

Some psychologists (for example, Haring *et al.* 1978) have identified various stages in learning and have emphasised that the acquisition of skills or knowledge is only the first step in learning, not the whole process. This can be illustrated by the example of learning to drive a car. Initially, the learner driver probably learns how to drive a particular vehicle, and is hesitant and cautious, moving jerkily at first (the *acquisition stage* of learning). With time, the learner driver becomes more smooth and less jerky (the *fluency stage*). Then, with more time and practice, the learner driver is able to drive different makes and models of car (the *generalisation stage*) and to cope with driving with a broken arm or driving on the continent (the *adaptation stage*). Some people seem to go through these stages very rapidly and the four stages merge into one another as the learning takes place easily. For others, the process is long, slow and painful, with each stage having to be learned carefully and earlier steps having to be repeated and practised many times.

Teaching tends to focus on children's initial acquisition of knowledge and skills while relatively little attention is given to helping children to become fluent in these and in applying them to new contexts. Discussions about a broad curriculum for children who have difficulties in retaining learning must, therefore, include opportunities for later as well as initial stages of learning.

Developing fluency

One argument is that a child will only retain skills, concepts and knowledge when he or she has reached a particular level of fluency; that is, when the child can recall the information very rapidly. Most children reach this level quickly and easily but, for some, this is a long process which needs to be taught directly, just as some learner drivers have repeatedly to practise explicitly certain procedures (for example, looking into the mirror before moving off) before this becomes automatic (fluent).

Techniques to develop fluency have been suggested by various writers. These techniques include games and approaches such as precision teaching which involve brief, timed, mini-tests of learning a specific skill. For example, a child who can recall multiplication facts but is not quick in doing so, might play various snap-like games in order to speed up. An adult might give the child a short (perhaps only one-minute) test each day, which is presented as a game rather than as a formal test. The results from these mini-tests build up into a daily, then weekly, record of the number of multiplication facts recalled in each one-minute session.

As the child's fluency improves, results can be shown on a graph and this is encouraging to the child as he or she can see that progress is being made. If progress stops or slows then the adult needs to simplify the test. (See Haring *et al.* 1978, Levey and Branwhite 1987, Solity and Bull 1987, for discussion and examples of precision teaching techniques.) Simplified versions of this approach might involve a regular game in which the child works with an adult on a timed activity linked with the skill in which fluency is to be developed. Quick (timed) reading of a group of sight vocabulary words on small flashcards is one popular example.

Two important points from this work are that teachers need to have: (a) a way of checking, and recording, whether or not earlier knowledge and skills have been retained, (b) elements which are part of usual classroom activities and can be used to help children with learning difficulties to 'overlearn' skills and knowledge.

Using 'spare time'

Some teachers have systems of 'spare time' activities which they use for children with learning difficulties so that they practise using material that has been learned (i.e. acquired). This might be organised by having a convention or classroom rule about what children do in 'spare time', and some teachers display this timetable in the classroom. Such a 'spare time' activities timetable could be devised for individuals or groups. Table 3.1 is an example of how a teacher might plan 'spare time' activities for several year 3 children with reading difficulties.

Table 3.1 Spare time activities: sample timetable

	For Julie and Mark	For Lucy and Sally
MONDAY	Microcomputer game	Taped sounds quiz
TUESDAY	Taped sounds quiz	Words quiz (on LM*)
WEDNESDAY	Letter sounds games	Own choice
THURSDAY	Words quiz (on LM*)	Microcomputer game
FRIDAY	Own choice	Letter sounds games

*LM = *Language Master* machine

Speed games

Various 'speed' games can be developed in the classroom to encourage children with learning difficulties to keep practising and rehearsing skills and knowledge until they reach a level at which these are retained over the longer term. These speed games might involve children timing one another against a clock (for example, when rehearsing sight vocabulary words or number bonds). Clearly these types of game need to be used sensitively so that they foster, not hinder, children's learning. If the atmosphere of the game becomes too tense and competitive, it is likely to be counter-productive. Often parental help at home can be used to develop children's fluency. For example, in some local education authorities parents of children with moderate learning difficulties have been taught to use precision teaching techniques with their children. One advantage of such an approach is that the parents as well as the child can see that the child is maintaining skills. This kind of 'game' works best for relatively simple skills and should go alongside broader approaches to developing the child's learning.

Similarly, some microcomputer software programs can help children to rehearse specific skills or to apply knowledge in an interesting way. Publications from the National Council for Educational Technology (for example, NCET 1993, 1994a) and AVP (for example, AVP 1992) contain descriptions of relevant software. These programs can often be personalised and immediate positive feedback included (for example, smiley faces). The endless patience and unlimited questions from a microcomputer can, within limits, provide the sort of extensive practice which may otherwise not be found within usual class activities. If such practice is tied to a game format, then an individual child may obtain practice without this becoming tedious.

The need to maintain fluency in skills and knowledge is not specific to the National Curriculum. However, the importance of the National Curriculum means that associated record sheets for children with learning difficulties should aim to include notes about fluency as well as regular checks to see that knowledge and skills have been retained. Teachers are likely to be particularly aware of this at the reporting ages, usually years 2 and 6, when continuous teacher assessments and results on end of key stage assessment tests and tasks will be reported. The importance, for children with learning difficulties, of 'over-learning' knowledge and skills is illustrated in the following example.

An example: Wesley

Wesley was a 9-year-old who could write a couple of short sentences but seemed unable to progress to writing stories or accounts without a great deal of help from the teacher. After talking through attempts at writing with Wesley, his teacher decided that the underlying difficulty was that Wesley, although he wanted to write, was unable to look up words quickly in a simple dictionary. Since she discouraged children from 'queueing' for words from her, and Wesley disliked asking other children for help, he had got into the habit of not writing very much in order to avoid the problem of going through, for him, a laborious process in order to locate the required word. Given time and structured help, Wesley could find words in the dictionary but he could not do this quickly on his own.

The teacher was involved in staff discussions to analyse the intermediate goals involved in being able to use a simple dictionary (discussed in Lewis 1985). From this, a range of games was devised to help children to over-learn alphabetical order. Wesley enjoyed these games and often chose to do them (for example, during 'wet' playtimes). He became more confident about finding words on his own. The games were only one element of classroom activities designed to foster dictionary use. They did seem to help Wesley to make the transition from faltering and cautious use of his own word book (containing words written by the teacher) to a wider and effective use of various classroom word books, lists and dictionaries.

Providing children with opportunities to generalise and adapt knowledge, concepts and skills

An important aspect of developing learning for children with difficulties is ensuring that those children have opportunities to use knowledge and skills in new contexts. Being able to add up numbers is of limited use if this can only be done using a particular set of blocks; the ability to read certain words is of restricted use if those words are only recognised in one context (for example, in a specific reading book). Topic-based approaches to the curriculum can be used to help children to apply knowledge, concepts and skills. A child who can add numbers up to 100 can be helped to generalise and adapt this ability by using it, for example, when devising a boardgame in which players add numbers on a modified die (its sides labelled, say, 32, 17, 23, etc.), or when making a model involving, say, finding two pieces of balsa-wood to glue together to make a plane wing of 300 mm in length.

Some children find it hard to adapt or apply knowledge to new situations. For example, some children do not realise, unless it is explicitly pointed out, that the following tasks require the same piece of mathematical knowledge:

(*spoken*)
• Two and five makes . . .
• Two plus five equals . . .
• A 2p coin and a 5p coin make . . .
• A 2 m piece of wood added to a 5 m piece of wood gives me a piece of wood . . . m long.
(*written*)
• $2 + 5 =$
• $5 + 2 =$
• $(2, 5)$
• $2 + 5$
• $2 + 5 = \square$
• $\boxed{2} + \boxed{5} = \square$
• $2 +$
  5
  ___

  ___
• $5 + 2$
• $5 +$
  2
  ___

  ___
• $2p + 5p =$
• $2 \text{ kg} + 5 \text{ kg} =$

Similarly, different print or handwriting styles (for example, A, a, ℛ, 𝒜, and 𝒜) may not be interpreted as representing the same letter.

In the same way, a child with difficulties in learning may understand that his or her runner bean needs water to grow. However, if the child is then asked about what a lemon pip or an oak tree needs to grow, or if the question is turned round and the child is asked, 'If we stop watering the bean what will happen?', then the child may be confused and unable to answer. These questions require the child not just to understand the one instance but also to be able to extrapolate the general rule and apply it to relevant situations. It is at this point that learning may stop, perhaps because the teacher has assumed that the child, having understood the first instance, will have made the connection with an understanding of the general rule. Consequently, teaching plans for children who have difficulties in learning need to include the developing of generalisation and the adaptation of skills and knowledge. This has always been an important, although sometimes overlooked, aspect of children's learning.

End of key stage assessment tests and tasks may probe, not just skills and understanding acquired, but the child's ability (a) to apply those skills and knowledge to novel situations and/or (b) to recognise the known in an unfamiliar format. The following example, from a series of assessment tasks for 7-year-olds (Jones *et al.* 1989), illustrates the confusion which might arise for a child with difficulties when given a simple but 'disguised' task:

Stripey and Curly go on a picnic with 2 friends, Flip and Flop.

(a) The 4 friends take 2 sandwiches each.
    How many sandwiches are there altogether?

(b) They share a bag of 20 sweets between them and
    have the same number of sweets each.
    How many sweets do they each have?

(Activity booklet, *The Picnic*, pp. 2–3)

Task (a) is asking: what is 4 x 2? A child with difficulties in mathematics might be able to do the multiplication but might not recognise that this is what is required in (a). Similarly (b) might not be recognised as asking: 20 divided by 4 = ?

This is an illustration of how a child who is competent on readily recognisable number tasks might appear to lack these skills because he or she fails to recognise the need to apply the particular skill(s). (Other issues concerning end of key stage assessment tests and tasks with children who have learning difficulties are explored in Chapter 10.)

It is not being suggested here that teachers should have prescriptive lists of generalisation/adaptation activities through which children with learning difficulties work. Topic work can provide naturally many opportunities for children to practise skills and to demonstrate whether or not skills and knowledge can be generalised and applied. This is illustrated in the following example of one child's difficulties.

An example: Kate

Kate was an 8-year-old with difficulties in reading. She had a small sight vocabulary but this was limited to recognising the words in her home-made reading book. She read fluently the whole sentences in the book and the individual words when these were shown separately, using *Breakthrough* sentence makers. Kate wanted a second reading book but her teacher was hesitant about going on as Kate was unable to recognise the words from her first book when they appeared elsewhere, such as in classroom notices. Kate seemed to have acquired an initial level of skill and was fluent in this fairly limited area, but could not generalise it to other contexts.

Kate enjoyed activities using machines, so the teacher made *Language Master* cards of the individual words from Kate's book. At about this time, Kate's mother had another baby and Kate was keen to draw and talk about this. The teacher encouraged Kate to make a 'baby book' containing a great variety of relevant pictures and information. This was not specifically a reading book but Kate, while making the baby book, independently copied relevant words from her first reading book on to appropriate pages of her baby book. She had used the *Language Master* cards to check that these were the words she wanted. She had pasted into the book some christening cards and it was these that seemed to help Kate to recognise that 'baby' could be written in various colours, scripts, etc. but still say 'baby'. The teacher believed that this was the first time that Kate had recognised for herself the generalis-ability of one of her sight vocabulary words. The teacher then made a class newspaper on which various items of news were written. Kate's baby news was included in this and from this point Kate began to recognise firstly her baby book words and then her reading book words in other contexts.

CONCLUSION

This and the preceding chapters have reviewed issues and practice concerning breadth in the curriculum. The following chapter examines one of the fundamental topics in all teaching, but one which is of especial importance if children have difficulties in learning: that of identifying 'where children are at' in their learning.

Chapter 4

Identifying the point reached by the child

It is a truism that learning must start from the point at which the child is; how could it be otherwise? What is harder to achieve in practice is that teaching begins from where the child is or, to put it another way, that teaching matches the child's learning needs. This stance is endorsed in the Code of Practice concerning special educational needs (DFE 1994a) which states that 'At the heart of every school and every class lies a cycle of planning, teaching and assessing' (para. 2.1).

The National Curriculum can be seen as one way of fostering this matching of child and curriculum. Early documentation about end of key stage assessment emphasised the links between teaching, learning and assessment (SEAC 1990a). Later announcements and materials (for example, Shephard 1994) have made a stronger distinction between continuous teacher assessment, to be linked to teaching (i.e. formative assessment), and summative assessments, made at the ends of key stages, explicitly for reporting purposes. Caroline Gipps (1994) has drawn attention to the differences between 't.a.' (non-moderated teacher assessment, used for formative purposes, or just within the classroom), 'T.A.' (moderated teacher assessment used for reporting purposes outside the classroom) and external tests. This chapter focuses on the first of these three types of classroom assessments of children's learning: continuous formative assessment. The second two types of assessment, used primarily for reporting purposes, are discussed in Chapter 10.

ESTABLISHING STARTING POINTS FOR LEARNING

If a child (or adult) has difficulty in learning something then the reaction of anyone inclined to take on the role of teacher is invariably to try to find out exactly what the learner can and cannot do. For example, someone trying to teach a friend (who has repeatedly failed the driving test) to drive, might well start by guessing the approximate level of the friend's driving ability and then asking the friend to perform certain manoeuvres (e.g. reversing, doing a three-point turn, making a hill start, negotiating a multi-storey car park). As a result of watching the attempts at these exercises, the teacher will note perhaps that gear changing is still awkward, so that more complex tasks are still inappropriate. Alternatively, it may be clear that the learner is over-confident and, given some slowing down, could complete the manoeuvres successfully. This example highlights a strategy which teachers in schools use, almost intuitively, when working with children with learning difficulties.

This strategy is the assessment of the learner through careful observation while he or she is engaged in attempts at the activity. It should be the starting point for all teaching but is sometimes lost as children are pushed onto the escalators of published schemes and swept along. Also, in a busy classroom, it is all too easy for continuous assessments of how children are learning to be replaced by quick assessments of the end-products.

An appropriate starting point for both further learning and the teacher's teaching is crucial for children (and adults) who find something difficult to learn. Most adults can recall something which they have found hard to 'pick up'; for example, learning to speak a foreign language, to play a musical instrument or to use a word processor. Sometimes difficulties can be traced to a teacher who 'started at the wrong place', assuming too much of the novice learner.

Assessments of children starting formal schooling

This section will consider ways in which the teacher might identify appropriate starting points in teaching for children who are finding tasks difficult. Advice and information from other teachers and the child's care-givers, in addition to careful observation of the child, can help to identify 'where the child is'. This is particularly important for children starting compulsory schooling, as the diversity of pre-infant school provision means that the reception class is likely to include 5-year-olds with widely

different experiences and expectations about school (this is discussed more fully in David and Lewis 1991). A group of primary
teachers with whom I discussed this identifed fourteen different
types of pre-school settings from which reception class children
may have come. Pre-reception class provision included infant
school class, nursery unit, nursery class, nursery school, playgroup, childminder, workplace crèche, family centre and home.

There is evidence that teachers at key stage 1 have tended to
make little use of assessment information passed on by staff in pre-
school settings attended by the child (Blyth and Wallace 1988).
This makes assessment of children near to the start of their infant
schooling particularly important if teaching is to be appropriately
matched to children's learning needs. An OFSTED survey of
urban schools found that, even after the introduction of the
National Curriculum, children's abilities were rarely assessed on
school entry and little use was made of available information to
plan teaching (OFSTED 1993a).

The diversity of educational experiences prior to key stage 1,
and how the reception class teacher might build on these experiences, raises issues about 'baseline' assessment of children at
the start of key stage 1 (Tizard *et al.* 1988, Nuttall and Goldstein
1989, Thomas 1989). The term 'baseline' assessment has been used
to refer to assessment near to the start of full-time compulsory
schooling. It has misleading connotations of children coming into
reception classes with minimal educational attainments, whereas
a wide variety of research (for example, Tizard *et al.* 1988) has
shown the richness of experiences and attainments which children
have on starting formal schooling. It has been argued that
including National Curriculum assessments on school entry provides a sound and sensible base from which to monitor children's
progress on the National Curriculum. This is important because
of the diversity of children's pre-school experiences.

Value-added notions

Those in favour of assessing children at school entry on National
Curriculum-related targets argue that this provides a measure
against which to assess children's attainments at age 7. This
argument draws heavily on marketing notions of 'value added' to
a product. Roasted coffee beans sell for (hypothetically) x for

500 grammes; ground, roasted coffee beans sell for x times 2; ground, roasted, vacuum-packed coffee beans sell for x times 3. Successive stages add value (for the manufacturer and retailer) in terms of how much the customer will pay. Adding value costs the manufacturer something but the more that 'value' is added, the higher the potential profit. In the educational context it is said that assessments of value added would distinguish between a school which has initially high-attaining pupils, who nevertheless make relatively little further progress over the next few years in school, and a school which receives a relatively low-attaining intake but makes great progress with these children. The former school has added little 'value'; the latter school has added high 'value'. However the latter school may, in terms of reported attainments at age 7, appear to be less successful than the former 'high intake' school. Since the introduction of the National Curriculum there have been attempts to measure value added, mainly focusing on the secondary school age range.

Derek Haylock (1994) makes the interesting point that it is really value multiplied for which the school should get credit. He argues that the schoool does not deserve three times as much credit for, for example, moving a child from level 3 to level 6 (increase of three levels), as for moving a child from level 1 to level 2 (increase of 1 level). In his value-multiplied approach, the credit for the first case (moving a child from level 3 to level 6) would be 2 (i.e. 3 (initial level) × 2 = 6 (final level). The credit for the second case (moving a child from level 1 to level 2) would also be 2 (i.e. 1 (initial level) × 2 = 2 (final level). So the school would obtain as much credit for small progress by an initially low-attaining child, as for greater progress from an initially higher-attaining child. This has at face value a fairness which simpler value-added approaches lack. However, it intensifies a dangerous disadvantage. If we are able to arrive at some agreed way of measuring the value that a school has added to pupils' learning then teachers are more likely to be held directly to blame where 'value added' or 'value multiplied' appears comparatively low. This is justified when it reflects factors within the school's control, such as teaching processes. However, it is conceivable that comparatively little 'value added/multiplied' will reflect factors over which the school has no control or factors which have been omitted from the formulation of 'value added/multiplied'.

Approaches

Since the introduction of the National Curriculum some local education authorities and individual schools have brought in baseline assessment for 5-year-olds. These assessments divide into the following broad types (some of which are used in combination):

1 those planned around the National Curriculum explicitly; for example, identifying elements of level 1 attainment targets in the core areas (unpublished materials on these lines have been produced by, among others, Sussex, Warwickshire and Northamptonshire local education authorities);
2 those based on sub-divisions of specific early learning activities or tests (such as the *Real Reading Analysis*, Bostock *et al.* 1990);
3 those utilising checklists based on classroom observation (such as the *Bury Infant Check*, Pearson and Quinn 1986, or the *Infant Rating Scale*, Lindsay 1981);
4 those based on guided observations referenced to developmental scales (such as the *Keele Pre-school Assessment Guide*, Tyler 1980) and
5 those centring on interviews with, or reports by, care-givers or the children themselves (for example, *All About Me*, Wolfendale 1989).

Some of those in the first category have been circulated informally. Few have yet been published or distributed outside the local education authorities in which they have been developed. Anecdotal evidence suggests that a great deal of teachers' time and energies have gone into developing these baseline assessment procedures but many have subsequently been abandoned as too time consuming. Peter Blatchford and Tony Cline (Blatchford and Cline 1992, Cline and Blatchford 1994) have discussed the general principles behind the evaluation of baseline assessments. These principles relate to:

• theoretical integrity (for example, is the underlying model of children's development or the model of the curriculum based on satisfactory evidence?);
• practical efficacy (for example, is the information valid and reliable?);
• equity (for example, are children's rights adequately protected?);

- accountability (for example, is the measure cost-effective?).

In the longer term we also need to know how these types of assessment link with progress in the National Curriculum and other aspects of the child's curriculum.

Those who are opposed to baseline assessments at age 5, in relation to the National Curriculum, maintain that this will label some children as 'failures' from their first days in school. It is also said that assessment results will eventually be linked in an undesirable way with teacher appraisal, reflecting a return to a covert payment-by-results system. More fundamentally, some of those who have argued against National Curriculum-linked assessment on school entry hold that this would be contrary to the basic principles of early childhood education (for example, Bruce 1987), which emphasise acceptance of children's individuality and an avoidance of crude assessments of children's abilities in terms of products of learning. Linked with these two last points is the argument that such young children cannot be assessed in these terms in ways which are valid and reliable.

These divergent views reflect contrasting ideas about the purposes of this 'baseline' assessment. The 'value-added' arguments imply a prime concern with accountability: attainments at age 5 are only made in order to provide a comparison with attainments at age 7. A second purpose, in the special needs context, and one which was advocated in the 1970s, was assessment at age 5 in order to identify children thought likely to have later difficulties in learning. This psychological orientation hinged on the predictive validity of the tests used and is still being debated. It was argued that if it can be 'proved' that, for example, not being able to read letter-sounds at age 5 predicts being a poor reader at age 7, then all children should be tested on letter sound knowledge at age 5. In practice, if teachers think that a child will find reading difficult, then they try to prevent this. Consequently, attempts to use attainments at age 5 predictively have often been confounded (rightly) by practice. For most teachers, the purpose of assessment, interpreted broadly, of children starting school is to make teaching more effective by getting to know a whole range of things about each child and where he or she is in his or her learning. Increasingly, information from parents and care-givers has been integrated into the school's formal (Wolfendale 1989) and informal (David and Lewis 1991) assessment procedures. This trend is likely to be sharpened by the Code of Practice on the identification and assessment of special educational needs (DFE 1994a) which states that 'effective assessment and provision will be secured where there is the greatest possible degree of partnership between parents and their children and schools' (para. 1.2).

What I am advocating in this chapter is careful assessment, through various forms of observation (not formal tests) of the point reached by a child in his or her learning, and teaching which builds on this knowledge. It is not being suggested that starting points for, say, 5-year-olds should be only in terms specifically and directly linked with National Curriculum attainment targets. Broader assessment based on observation is important for all children but particularly for any children thought to have difficulties in learning.

ASSESSMENT OF 'ACTUAL' OR 'POTENTIAL' LEARNING?

Learning potential has been a very seductive topic in education and among its victims are the writers of some of the National Curriculum circulars. For example, Circulars 6/89 and 2/90 (DES 1989d, 1990b) contain an identical paragraph stating that: 'Schools should bear in mind that the objective of the National Curriculum is to ensure that each pupil should obtain maximum benefit, by stretching the pupil to reach his or her potential, but without making impossible demands' (paras 58 and 33 respectively). Similarly, Circular 22/89 (DES 1989e) refers to 'cultural differences' masking the child's 'true learning potential' (para. 88). Both sets of statements are about not expecting too little of children. This is an important point but the argument is hampered by referring to 'potential' as if children are recalcitrant elastic bands. Assessments of 'potential' are impossible, as no one can *know* another's potential. All we can make are best guesses (as valid and reliable as possible) which give a partial view of some current attainments and attitudes.

FORMATIVE TEACHER ASSESSMENT AND THE CODE OF PRACTICE

The Code of Practice (DFE 1994a) sets out five stages through which the assessment of a child thought to have special educational needs may move. The stages are not compulsory but the Code describes each stage as a guide to help schools monitor such children's needs and progress. The first three stages are based within the school and are relevant to discussion in this chapter about formative teacher assessments of children with special educational needs.

Stage 1

This stage of assessment is organised by the school. Stage 1 is initiated by a teacher at the school, a parent or another professional, expressing concern about the child's learning. This person should have some evidence to back up this expression of concern. The class teacher responds to this expression of concern by gathering relevant information, consulting the school's co-ordinator for special educational needs, consulting the parents and taking action to prevent early signs of difficulties from escalating. The Code lists the types of information required at stage 1. These are:

- class records;
- National Curriculum attainments;
- standardised test results or profiles;
- records of achievement;
- reports on the child in school settings;
- observations about the child's behaviour;
- parental views on the child's health and development;
- parental perceptions of the child's progress and behaviour;
- parental views about possible factors contributing to the child's difficulties;
- parental views about action the school might take;
- the child's perceptions of his/her difficulties;
- the child's views about how difficulties might be addressed;
- relevant information from other sources, such as medical or health or social services.

(DFE 1994a: 24)

The school's coordinator for special educational needs should ensure that the child's name is included in the school's special needs register. This register is a requirement introduced through the 1993 Education Act and subsequent Code. The child's progress should be re-examined after at least two 'review periods'. The

Code suggests that the first review 'might be within a term' (DFE 1994a: 25).

Stage 2

This stage of assessment is also organised by the school. A child might be placed at stage 2 because either stage 1 assessments show continuing concern or, although the child has not gone through stage 1, the coordinator for special educational needs considers that early intensive action is necessary. A similar range of information to that given at stage 1 is needed. In addition, the coordinator for special educational needs should seek information from medical and social services. Information may be sought, with the parents' consent, from the child's GP. Review arrangements are similar to those for stage 1. The school's coordinator for special educational needs should ensure that an individual education plan is drawn up (see DFE 1994a: 26–9). This plan is worked out in collaboration with the class teacher.

Stage 3

This stage of assessment is also organised by the school. At this stage the school calls on external specialist support to help the child make progress. The new individual education plan, drawn up by the coordinator, should (like the individual education plan at stage 2) include information on the child's learning difficulties, action to be taken, help to be provided at home, learning targets to be achieved, pastoral or medical care requirements, monitoring and assessment arrangements, and review arrangements (see DFE 1994a: 29–34).

Many of the strategies described in this chapter will be valuable before a child is registered as being at stage 1. There is little point in delaying such assessments just because the child has not formally been noted as being at stage 1 or beyond. The strategies and techniques will be central to assessments made by the school for children thought to be at stages 1, 2 or 3. The approaches described are also pertinent to stages 4 and 5 which is when the local education authority becomes involved. The school will then have to provide detailed evidence to the local education authority about the educational programmes used with the child and the monitoring of those programmes. At stage 4 the local education authority considers the need for a statutory assessment and at stage 5 it considers whether the child needs a formal statement of special educational needs (see DFE 1994a: 38–123).

ASSESSMENTS THROUGH CLASSROOM OBSERVATION

Observation of children is a vital first step in planning how their learning can be fostered. Observation can take many forms, structured or unstructured, involving the teacher working with the child or remaining distanced. When and how teachers observe children will depend both on the aims of that observation and on what is realistic in a busy classrooom. While teachers recognise that watching how children are learning is an important part of teaching (and this is a particularly strong tradition in the early years of schooling), it requires careful planning to incorporate such activity into everyday classroom life.

Teachers may make time for observing children by doing more collaborative teaching in which one teacher takes the main responsibility for two class groups while the other teacher observes or works closely with a small group. Similarly, other classroom adults can be utilised (for example, trainee teachers) so that a class teacher has observation time. A variety of occasions arising unexpectedly (for example, in the playground) may provide the opportunity for informal observational assessments. Adults, other than the teacher, might also carry out the observations if given clear and detailed training about how to do this. I have worked with nursery nurses in primary schools who, using structured observation schedules, have monitored the integration of children from special schools (discussed further later). Similar work is described in accounts of Sunnyside Primary School's experiences of integration (Bell and Colbeck 1989). This type of work can generate valuable data about whether or not children with difficulties in learning are isolated in mainstream school classes and about the types of activities in which they are engaged.

The following discussion considers various approaches to continuous teacher assessments of children's development and learning, from relatively informal approaches to more formal and child-specific methods. Although they are of general relevance, they are particularly important in the planning of teaching and learning for children with difficulties for whom classroom work often seems to be mismatched.

General classroom observations

A variety of general observations helps the teacher to get to know individual children. For example:

- In which kinds of activity does the child concentrate better or less well? What are typical periods of concentration for the child on particular activities?
- Which kinds of activity seem to be most meaningful for the child?
- In which kinds of activity is the child most confident?
- Does the child have a preference for certain kinds of materials (for example, microcomputer-based or linked with a particular piece of equipment such as a synchrofax or *Language Master* machine)?
- Does the child work better at certain times of the day (for example, always tired in the first part of the morning or regularly livelier after the midday break)?
- Are there particular classroom friends with whom the child works well or poorly?
- What motivates the child to learn?
- What special interests does the child have?
- In which kinds of classroom grouping does the child work better or less well?
- Does the child prefer a noisy or quiet working environment?
- How does the child respond if given scope for developing his or her own ideas?

All of these things relate to getting to know the child and, once identified, they can be built on positively so that the classroom fosters rather than hampers learning. In the longer term, children who favour a particular learning style (for example, using computer-based materials) will need to have experience in using other approaches also.

The importance of motivation in influencing what children are apparently capable of is illustrated in the following account. A 7-year-old, Sarah, seemed unable to write even a sentence towards a story or 'news'. However, one day Sarah received a party invitation from a friend, Marie, in another class. She took the invitation home and showed it to her father, who wrote a reply saying that Sarah could come to the party. Sarah lost this note on her way to school the next day and became very upset about this. Her class teacher reassured her, saying that it would be all right as she would pass on the message to Marie's teacher for her to give to Marie. However, later that day Sarah handed her teacher a carefully written note saying: 'To Marie, I am coming to your party. From Sarah.' Sarah had written the note and may have had help from other children with spellings but, highly anxious not to miss the party, she had been prompted to write a message. The message had a real purpose and brought out her writing abilities.

A class teacher probably cannot individualise learning to such an extent that, even if he or she knows how every child responds to the features listed above, the class can be organised on this basis. However, knowing how children respond to different situations and discussing this with the children's care-givers will help the teacher to make informed decisions about classroom organisation. These general observations may alert the teacher to possible hearing or visual impairments in a child.

Stages 1–3: observation as a guide to sensory or physical impairments

Sensory impairments, perhaps mild or transitory, may underlie or compound difficulties in learning. If a child cannot see his or her work clearly or cannot hear instructions clearly then it is likely that what the child does will appear to be 'wrong'. There is a wide range of cues which might convey to an observer that the child has hearing difficulties. These include the child:

- appearing to ignore the teacher's questions;
- having a frequent lack of attention in oral activities;
- having difficulty in following directions;
- depending on classmates for instructions;
- tilting his or her head at an angle to hear a sound;
- having speech difficulties (particularly omitting word beginnings or endings);
- having frequent ear infections;
- sitting close to the TV or radio;
- doing badly on auditory discrimination games such as identifying rhyming words;

- talking with a very loud voice;
- being conspicuously more able in a one-to-one situation than when participating in a large group;
- appearing to forget instructions.

It has been estimated that approximately one in every ten young children has some hearing impairment; so it is possible, especially at the infant school stage, that learning difficulties will be related to hearing difficulty. If a teacher suspects that a child does have a hearing impairment then formal audiometric testing can be requested. An interim stage might be to give the child a simple individual hearing test requiring the child to identify a particular picture from a group of pictures with similar sounding names (e.g. cap, fan, cat, lamb). The Royal National Institute for the Deaf (RNID) has produced spiral-bound books of relevant pictures, carefully selected so that consistent errors will highlight particular types of hearing difficulty; for example, those concerning low-frequency sounds (RNID 1970).

Similarly, the observant teacher can pick up a number of cues indicating visual difficulties in a child. These cues include the child:

- complaining of aches in the eye(s) especially after long periods of close work;
- rubbing his or her eyes vigorously;
- closing or covering one eye;
- showing sensitivity to light;
- complaining about reflections from whiteboards or black-boards;
- holding reading materials very close to, far from, or at an odd angle to, the eyes;
- sitting close to the TV/computer screen;
- squinting or frowning when doing close work;
- complaining of blurred vision;
- varying attainments reflecting the size of the print in material used by the child;
- confusing letters/numerals of similar shape;
- having recurrent inflammation of the eyes;
- having poor handwriting;
- avoiding, or poor at, detailed observational drawing;
- finding difficult a variety of fine hand–eye coordination tasks.

Colour blindness can easily pass unnoticed. One teacher I met told me of how her son, after a successful and happy few years in an infant school, had many problems on transferring to the junior school. It emerged that the junior school, unlike the infant school, used green chalkboards and her son could not distinguish clearly between the board writing and the green background. This had led him to avoid class work and to make many errors when he did attempt it. Neither she nor the previous school had suspected that her son was colour blind, although subsequent tests showed that he had red–green colour blindness, hence the particular problems with green chalkboards. Presumably such children would have similar difficulties with certain combinations of worksheet/workcard and ink colours. If visual difficulties are suspected then formal eye testing can be requested.

It is worth noting that a history of hearing or visual difficulties at the pre-infant school stage might be reflected in poor language or graphic skills in the infant school. Pre-infant school records and discussions with care-givers help to identify earlier difficulties. Of course, the presence of sensory impairments does not necessarily mean that the child will have (or have had) difficulties in learning.

Further information about identifying and responding to sensory difficulties can be found in SNAP (Ainscow and Muncey 1984), TIPS (Dawson 1985) and ATL (1994) materials. The RNID and RNIB, as well as other charitable foundations (see Male and Thompson 1985), will also give advice.

Teachers, especially at key stage 1, may also be the first people outside the family to notice a child's physical difficulties. It has been estimated that about 6 per cent of children between ages 6 and 11 are unusually clumsy. This is termed developmental coordination disorder (Henderson and Sugden 1992, Sugden and Henderson 1994, Dussart 1994). One or two children in a mainstream primary class might show signs of a lack of physical coordination and consequently poor motor skills. Possible signs of a developmental coordination disorder include:

- delay in childhood developmental milestones such as sitting, crawling, and walking;
- starting school lacking physical competencies attained by peers, such as dressing self, climbing stairs and playground equipment, feeding self, and handling crayons correctly;
- showing frustration with physical tasks such as pouring liquids, measuring, cutting out, threading objects, drawing, and writing.

If sensory or physical difficulties are suspected then liaison with care-givers and the school's coordinator for special educational needs about the issue is very important. If evidence about suspected difficulties is collected by care-givers and teachers then health professionals have a useful supplement to medical diagnosis. This broader picture may help to rule out non-medical factors influencing behaviour. For example, a child may show fear in physical education activities in school. If this goes alongside coordination problems at school and at home then resultant action will differ from that in which this does not happen and fearfulness in school PE seems more related to a lack of self-confidence.

Strategies for responding to developmental coordination difficulties include pairing the child with a better coordinated friend, teaching the child to talk himself or herself through the task and providing prepared layouts (Gross 1993).

Mainstream teachers may also have to respond to a range of children's medical problems, notably asthma, epilepsy and diabetes. A recent asthma awareness campaign has suggested that teachers should not, as has apparently been common practice in many schools, keep inhalers in a 'safe place' which is inaccessible to the children. Instead children who may need inhalers should have ready access to these at all times. Work by Michael Bannon and his co-workers (1992) showed that few teachers had received information about childhood epilepsy and they lacked confidence in dealing with children's epilepsy. However, the teachers had a good general knowledge of this condition and adequate awareness of the likely difficulties experienced by a child with epilepsy. The authors concluded that local health authorities have an important role to play in providing appropriate training packages for teachers. There are a number of publications outlining the implications for teachers of children's medical conditions (for example, ATL 1994).

Stages 1–5: systematic observation

It may be appropriate to carry out some systematic observations of children, using structured observation schedules. Sue Roffey and her co-workers (1994) identify four means of structuring classroom observations. These strategies are: making a tally, taking field notes, using a checklist, or monitoring behaviour at times intervals. The latter involves recording children's activities, using a schedule based on prespecified lists or categories of observed behaviours, often monitored over regular time periods (for example, every 30 seconds). The use of these schedules was noted earlier in relation to using different adults to make classroom observations. Systematic schedules are particularly useful for monitoring social behaviour. They can also be useful when monitoring a group of children in order to ascertain, for example, which children in the group contribute most to the conversation.

The following approach (adapted from Sylva *et al.* 1980) was used by staff in several schools who were monitoring the kinds of classroom interaction in which children with severe learning difficulties in primary schools were involved. A similar, but more tightly structured, example of this approach was used in the PACE project which investigated the impact of the National Curriculum at key stage 1 (see Pollard *et al.* 1994). The approach could be adapted for a variety of situations and aims.

1 Decide which children you want to observe and why.
   Let other staff know who these children are and when you will be observing them. You might decide to focus on a small number of children, observing each child in turn.
2 Prepare a sheet on which to record your observations. Draw horizontal lines to demarcate each one-minute time band.
3 Observe for several minutes before you start to make notes.
4 Observe each target child in turn for five minutes.
5 Write down:
   (a) What the child says (language);
   (b) With whom the child interacts (social);
   (c) What the child does (activity).
   This should be factual not interpretative.
   Do this for each one-minute band.
6 Afterwards, code each of the three sections. The codings will be specific to the context but might include:
   (a) REQ (request);
       PS (personal statement).
   (b) SOL (solitary);
       INA (interacting with adult);
       INC (interacting with another child).
   (c) TT (teaching a task to another child).

7   The results could then be put on to a graph or chart to show, for example, the proportion of time that the child(ren) is/are involved in solitary activities.

8   If possible, have two adults make observations simultaneously on the same child(ren). This will help to show whether or not the observations are reliable.

9   Consider the implications, for classroom practice, of what has been observed.

10   Consider repeating the observation exercise, with any necessary amendments to the original schedule.

There are both strengths and disadvantages in using structured, systematic observation schedules within a classroom. If the schedule is clearly structured and appropriate for the aims then it can supply useful information. It can show whether or not a teacher's impression is justified; for example, that a particular child habitually concentrates much better on oral than on written activities, or that two children work more productively together than separately. However, a structured observation schedule may be difficult to use effectively. Children may interrupt or behave differently because they are aware of being monitored. The use of structured observation schedules also requires at least two adults to be present, one to carry out the observations and one to work with the class. Several detailed accounts of formal observational methods (for example, Croll 1986, Slee 1987, Sylva and Neill 1990, Wragg 1993) expand on their use in classrooms.

Observational methods are useful ways in which teachers can build up judgements about individual children and the dynamics of the classroom. They may also point to features of the classroom which the teacher could improve, such as making certain types of resources more accessible (discussed in Chapter 8) or changing the location of some materials so that withdrawn children become more involved with other children. So far in this chapter, identifying the point reached by a child has focused on observations of children's general development and behaviour. Observational methods need to be supplemented with assessments which focus on curricular tasks. The SEAC (1990a) materials on teacher assessment provide many pointers for ways in which this can be done across the ability range. The next part of this chapter considers curriculum-based assessment in relation to children with difficulties in learning.

STAGES 1–3: ASSESSMENTS THROUGH CHILD–ADULT CONFERENCES

It is useful if the teacher can observe a child both working alone on a particular activity and working alongside the teacher. This is important because it enables the teacher to assess, first, the processes of learning and not just the end-products and, second, what the child can do alone compared with what he or she can do with some guidance. This kind of activity is described in the report from the task group on assessment and testing (DES/WO 1988) and in National Curriculum-linked assessment materials (SEAC 1990a).

I watched a 6-year-old boy, Sanjit, carrying out some work on making a block graph to show the numbers of children in the class staying for school dinner, eating a packed lunch or going home. Sanjit moved around the classroom with a sheet of paper on which there were three columns, depicting each of these choices. Sanjit asked each child which category he or she was in and then that child placed a tick in the appropriate column. Sanjit transferred the information from the ticked columns to a sheet of squared paper to produce a block graph containing the three sets ('school dinners', 'packed lunch' and 'home'). Sanjit completed the first two bars correctly on his own and I thought that he had done this by counting the number of ticks in each column and then counting up the same number of squares to produce the bar. However, when I talked to Sanjit about drawing the third bar, it became clear that he was not counting the ticks to determine the length of the bar but was using one-to-one matching to produce bars of the correct height. These two strategies (one-to-one matching and counting) have different implications for helping Sanjit to make the next step in his understanding.

Alistair McIntosh (1978) has recorded an interesting series of responses from 7- to 11-year-olds when asked to explain how they worked out the answer to '431 – 145 =' (written horizontally). All the children had provided the correct answer to this sum. Some children when asked to explain how they had arrived at their answer could not provide an explanation and said things like 'I thought of it in my head' or 'I guessed the answer'. Other children used decomposition methods:

5 take away 1, can't do it. Borrow 1 from 3. Cross the 3 out. Put 2 at the top. Then 11 take away 5 is 6. 2 take away 4, can't do it.

Borrow 1 from the 4. Put the 3 on top. 12 take away 4 is 8. 3 take away 1 is 2.

A few children used equal addition:

Can't take 5 from 1 so you have to borrow 1. 5 from 11 equals 6. Give the one back. So its 5 from 3, can't so you borrow 1, 5 from 13 leaves 8. Pay the 1 back, 2 from 4 is 2.

One child used complementary addition:

1 added 5 to 145 = 150, add 50 = 200, add 200 = 400, add 31 is 431, = 286.

Several children used idiosyncratic methods which they seemed to have devised for themselves:

I decided to take the hundreds away first. That was 300. I forgot those and rounded off the other numbers to the next 10 upwards. 50 from 300 is 250. Discard the hundreds and keep the 50. Now, because the 50 you took was really 45, add a 5 and the 1 from the 30 and then put them together with the 30. That makes 86. Now add the 100 and you get 286.

Take away the 100 which makes it 331, make it 300 and take 31 from the remaining 45, then take the answer (14) and take it away from 300 which makes the answer 286.

I took 100 from 400. I took 45 away from it. Then I added 31 on to it.

Similarly, a group of children working on addition of money might arrive at the correct answer in different ways. Asked to add 12p and 8p (whether in the context of playing in a class shop, using workcards or worksheets or playing a game), children could arrive at the correct answer by counting on in ones (with or without coins or other materials), adding 12 and 8 as 'wholes', or adding 10 and 5 and then adding the remaining 2 and 3 respectively to make 20 (with or without coins). The different strategies used would suggest different types of activity to foster the next step in their learning. These examples show that talking to a child about how a task has been carried out can be very important even if the child has arrived at an appropriate answer. It is more usual for teachers, who are inevitably very busy in the classroom, to carry out this interviewing process only when children have made obvious errors.

Several writers have drawn attention to the importance of teachers 'interviewing' children as they work, to monitor the children's learning strategies. Various terms have been used for this type of activity, including 'TIC' (Teacher interaction with the child; Hunter-Carsch ·1990), tutorial dialogue (Meadows and Cashdan 1988), 'analytical interviews' (Bennett *et al.* 1984) and diagnostic teaching (for example, Stott 1978). I am using the term 'child–adult conferences' because this emphasises the two-way sharing of information focusing on a specific activity.

Evidence from HMI reports (for example, DES 1978a, 1988) and individual research projects suggests that this kind of activity is rarely found in primary schools. One study of 4-year-olds in school noted:

> Diagnosis of children's understandings were very noticeable by their absence, or were limited to brief encounters of an un-satisfactory kind . . . [Teachers] very rarely had to deem a task, or a child, a failure, since they were always able to find some aspect acceptable. It follows from this that almost every task could be judged a success, which is precisely what teachers did, irrespective of whether or not the child, or the work, had been seen.
>
> (Bennett and Kell 1989: 82)

This suggests that teachers do need to become more used to carrying out conferences with children to ascertain children's approaches to a task and whether or not learning towards specific goals is being promoted. Roger Beard (1987) suggests that it would be helpful for teachers to divert time from routinely hearing children read to carrying out less frequent, but more in-depth, reading interviews with children. The National Curriculum, with its emphasis on continuous teacher assessments, requires the kind of approach advocated by Roger Beard and others. Child–adult conferences are discussed here because they are central to identifying the points in learning that are reached by individual children.

The various approaches to child–adult conferencing give several pointers about how this may be done effectively in a primary school class.

Organising child–adult conferences

- Acknowledge that it will be done relatively infrequently but in some detail for individual children.
- Acknowledge that some children will need this more frequently than do other children.
- Discourage other children from interrupting the activity.
- Avoid handing over this task to other adults in the classroom unless they fully understand its purpose and how to carry it out.
- Making time for child–adult conferences will require that teachers make more use of techniques in which children work without direct teacher involvement (e.g. collaborative work with classmates and self-checking games).
- It may be useful to tape record the conference so that it can be analysed later. The tape will also provide evidence about the child's learning which could be kept as a record. Children often like to hear such tapes re-played and to comment on their learning and interaction with the teacher.
- Capitalise on occasions when the child is highly motivated and has a good relationship with the teacher, especially if this happens infrequently.

Key questions

- Can the child explain why he or she is carrying out an activity in a certain way?
- What can the child do alone, compared with prompting? This is also very important for identifying able children who are doing work well below that of which they are capable.
- What can the child do already on his or her own? (Teaching should extend not duplicate this.)
- Has the child retained earlier steps in learning? For example, a child who has difficulty in completing tens and units sums involving carrying might have forgotten the 'base 10' concept underlying the activity.
- Can the child complete a given task in one context and transfer it to another context (e.g. add numbers using beads on a string and using a number line)?
- Can the child apply knowledge and skills in a new context (e.g. multiply numbers in a maths game and use multiplication facts to work out the numbers of rulers needed by groups of children in an art activity)?

- Can the child respond to a variety of question types (e.g. questions requiring recall, evaluation, speculation, problem solving)? (For example, after a science activity: what happened when we . . . ? could it have been done in a better way . . . ? what might happen if we . . . ? how did you feel about . . . ?)
- Does the child understand what he or she is being asked to do? For example, does he or she understand the vocabulary of the teacher's question?

Will Swann (1988) gives a good example which illustrates this last point. He describes talking to a 5-year-old girl during her first week at school. The girl was drawing around flat, plastic shapes. He asked her, in the course of the conversation, how many sides the square had and in response the girl laid out, side by side, three other squares. He put them back and asked the girl to show him a side of a square. She pointed to the centre of the top surface of one square. He goes on to discuss the various and ambiguous contexts in which the girl may have come across the word 'side' (sides of a team, sitting side by side, the side of a cupboard, etc.) and conjectures that the girl's responses reflected her thinking through different meanings of 'side'. He concludes that the child's 'difficulty' with the task was largely illusory and that the real problem was a failure of communication on his part, and not the child's.

The ambiguity of teachers' talk, particularly in the reception class, when children may not have become socialised into school procedures and expectations, has been documented by Shirley Cleave and co-workers (1982) and by Mary Willes (1983). Both sets of research provide salutory reading, as they indicate the potential for misunderstandings in classrooms. Examples include a child who interpreted the teacher's instruction, 'Would you like to join the story group now', as an invitation ('no thank you') and children being confused by the ambiguities of the teacher's request for them to 'line up'. Children who find school learning difficult may be slower than other children to tune into the specific language conventions of the classroom. This point is considered further in Chapter 10 in connection with end of key stage assessment tasks.

Diagnostic assessment

There is a relatively strong tradition of child–adult conferences, in special needs contexts, for diagnostic purposes. This is illustrated in various approaches to assessing and helping children with reading difficulties. Child–adult conferences are widely supported in this context, although there are differing views about the best focus of the conference. Two contrasting foci have been strongly advocated. One focus, developed from formal testing of 'sub-skills', has been on the psychological sub-skills believed to underlie particular tasks, notably reading. Thus, for example, many 'reading readiness' tests have included assessments of the child's visual sequencing (for example, identifying the next letter(s) in a regular sequence), auditory sequencing (for example, recalling aural sequences of letters or numbers) and visual memory (for example, drawing from memory a shape shown briefly). The rationale was that reading was composed of discrete and identifiable sub-skills which could be isolated and measured. It then seemed logical to identify and remedy, by specific teaching, any weak sub-skills. Unfortunately, there was generally little transfer from resultant proficiency in the sub-skill(s) to facility in reading (see Adams 1990).

A different focus in child–adult conferences has been on analyses of children's errors in a particular activity. Systematic analyses of errors (or 'miscues') can provide useful clues for teaching. For example, there are different implications for teaching in the case of James, who repeatedly makes phonic errors in spellings (for example, 'storiz' for 'stories'), compared with Toni, who fails to apply a common spelling rule (for example, she writes 'storys' for 'stories', 'worrys' for 'worries', etc.). Miscue analyses have been discussed in detail in relation to spelling (Peters 1975), reading (Arnold 1982, Bostock *et al.* 1990), handwriting (Alston and Taylor 1987) and mathematics (Hughes 1986). How the teacher chooses on which errors to focus and how these are analysed will reflect his or her theories (possibly implicit) about the nature of the knowledge/skills and the processes of acquiring these.

CONCLUSION

This chapter has examined the importance of trying to identify where children are in their learning. Several possible foci and some ways of carrying out individual assessments have been discussed. Identifying children's starting points is the first step in planning teaching. Curriculum-based assessment is, in the contexts of the Code of Practice, the National Curriculum and past work in relation to children with difficulties in learning, part of a continuous cycle of teaching and assessment. For that reason, curriculum-based assessment is considered further in the following chapter.

Chapter 5

Differentiation

Helping children progress in the National Curriculum by planning intermediate learning goals

Differentiation has caught on like tent pegs in a hurricane. It has emerged as an area of concern and energy in all the major published studies into the implementation of the National Curriculum. A study by the NFER (Weston *et al*. 1992) found that half the primary schools investigated had conducted a curriculum audit, or review, into how the National Curriculum was being differentiated in the school. One school in six had organised whole school INSET programmes on differentiation. In addition, one school in five had set up a staff working party to look specifically at differentiation.

INTERPRETATIONS OF THE TERM 'DIFFERENTIATION'

The term differentiation, like 'love' and 'health', is used freely but is ill-defined. Margaret Peter (1992) in her opening editorial to a collection of nine papers on differentiation, concluded that,

> It would be a miracle (or an act of piracy) if some [definitions of differentiation given by the authors] had been identical. But they mainly reflect the assumption about differentiation . . . that differentiation is about meeting every child's learning needs so that each can share in the same curriculum, usually in the same schools.
>
> (Peter 1992: 5)

This is the interpretation used in this chapter. Underlying the apparently simple idea of differentiation are complexities about exactly why, what, as well as more simply, how, differentiation is to be achieved.

Why differentiate the curriculum?

Margaret Peter (1992) identifies four motives in pursuing differentiation: the ideology of equal opportunities (it is right to give
all children access to the same curriculum), professionalism (it is
part of the teacher's role to deliver the National Curriculum to all
pupils), cost effectiveness (it is not economic to produce individual and different curricula) and expediency (accountability
procedures mean that teachers have to demonstrate that virtually
all children are receiving the National Curriculum). These strands
permeate much discussion about differentiation.

Reasons for differentiating the curriculum have been re-cast by
Brahm Norwich (1993, 1994a). He notes that differentiation is not
just a simple empirical and technical matter of finding ways of
adapting teaching to learners' diversity. It is also a complex matter
of finding conceptual, evaluative and practical ways of resolving
tensions between basic human values. He has related views about
differentiation to differences in social values concerning equality
and individuality. Put simply, a belief that children with special
needs should be treated in fundamentally the same way as other
children (equality principle) may point to differentiating the way
a common task is accessed. According to this line of argument
minimal differentiation is required in the National Curriculum,
just good (however that is defined) teaching for all children. A
strong version of this stance would see any other sort of differentiation as a form of curricular apartheid, discriminating in an
undesirable way by excluding some children from the curriculum
received by the majority. Some headteachers of special schools
have described differentiation in their schools in terms which
emphasise similarities with mainstream schools:

> My predecessor [believed that] to give our kids more of
> mainstream wasn't very appropriate. [But I think] mainstream
> has failed our kids very often and what is needed is the
> opportunity again or the chance to have their entitlement and
> its a question of *doing it in a more appropriate way.*
> (Study reported in Lewis and Halpin 1994; emphasis added)

Interestingly, interviews with pupils in segregated special schools
have indicated that those pupils valued doing work similar to that
done by pupils in mainstream schools (Costley, in preparation).

The views by these pupils and the headteacher's comment (above) reflect an implicit belief in the importance of curricular equality.

Alternatively, some educators hold that children with special needs must, as a priority, have those individual needs met (individuality principle). Following this line of argument, what is being done for the majority (i.e. pupils without special needs) is of secondary importance. A strong form of this stance is that to differentiate in a less extensive way is to impose an inappropriate curricular uniformity. Some headteachers of special schools have taken this view and have described differentiation in their schools in terms which emphasise the special school's unique position in responding sensitively to the diverse and idiosyncratic needs of individual pupils:

> We have devised our own curriculum . . . The National Curriculum isn't the starting point if you like, it's what the child [is], where the child is and *what the child needs*.
>
> (Study reported in Lewis and Halpin 1994; emphasis added)

What is to be differentiated?

Why we want to differentiate the curriculum is inextricably linked with what we want to differentiate. If differentiation is about giving all children access to the same curriculum, then differentiation may emphasise various access routes, such as providing taped versions of written material for visually impaired children. Such differentiation is likely to emphasise differentiation of teaching methods and classroom approaches, referenced to common curricula. The roots of this approach can be seen in theoretical work linking knowledge and control in society. Knowledge is linked with power, so denial of access to high status knowledge becomes a denial of access to potential power. One outcome of this view is an emphasis on pupils in special schools participating in GCSE programmes. In contrast, if differentiation is primarily concerned with meeting individual needs then differentiation may be seen as needing to focus on different educational goals for some children compared with the majority. The latter has been termed radical differentiation (Lewis and Sammons 1994). Differentiation from this perspective is likely to emphasise differentiation of educational goals and, as a result, differentiation of objectives and, possibly, teaching methods.

EVIDENCE ABOUT DIFFERENTIATION OF
THE NATIONAL CURRICULUM

As noted in Chapter 1, mainstream teachers have been over-whelmingly supportive of the principle of a common National Curriculum for all children, including those with special educational needs. Consequently, differentiation has often focused on differentiation of teaching methods. Research into the introduction of the National Curriculum at key stages 1 and 2 has found that teachers were committed to meeting pupils' individual needs through differentiation of the common curriculum (Webb 1993, Pollard *et al*. 1994). The National Curriculum has been associated with an increase in teachers' awareness of the need for differentiation.

Rosemary Webb (1993) found that at key stage 2 differentiation was provided mainly through differentiation by outcome (for example, asking all children to write a story, the level of work produced reflecting individual capabilities). In addition, differentiation of activities for children with special educational needs was carried out through differentiation of support. Support work was done by part-time teachers, non-teaching assistants and/ or volunteer helpers. However there was not enough time or scope for differentiating the curriculum as much as teachers wished. Teachers at key stage 2 considered that the pace and volume of National Curriculum work was particularly stressful for children with special educational needs. These children tended to accumulate unfinished work and so had fewer opportunities to experience success (Webb 1993).

Teachers' concern with differentiation may reflect, and be reflected in, the focus of INSET. Nearly two-thirds of the 300 primary schools surveyed in 1994 had received INSET on differentiation and 50 per cent of the schools surveyed wanted (more) INSET on differentiation (Lewis 1995a). The teachers surveyed had mixed feelings about differentiation. It was named as a benefit of the National Curriculum for children with special educational needs by nearly 10 per cent of these teachers. Conversely, it was given as the main difficulty by 15 per cent of the teachers (Lewis 1995a). It is not possible to know whether these teachers had the same thing in mind when differentiation was described as both a benefit and a disadvantage. The ambivalence may reflect:

1 different aspects of differentiation (for example, varying

support (seen as beneficial) and varying input through graded materials (seen as disadvantageous));

2 different degrees of one type of differentiation (for example, grouping – varying work groups (seen as beneficial) and individual working (seen as disadvantageous));

3 a contrast between support for differentation in theory (seen as beneficial) and practice (seen as disadvantageous) and/or

4 differences in usage of the term 'differentiation'.

DIFFERENTIATION OF TEACHING GOALS

One way of visualising the whole school curriculum, including the curriculum for children with learning difficulties, is as a ladder in which broad steps are specified for all children. Within this broad ladder there are points at which, for some children and possibly for only some of the time, smaller intermediate rungs are needed. Like most analogies this ladder model has some weaknesses, such as an image of children's learning as necessarily hierarchical, clearly defined, and sequential. However, the ladder idea does emphasise the integration of curricula for all children, curricular progression and continuity. It also fits with the broad concept of eight levels of attainment (plus one level for 'exceptional performance') embodied in the National Curriculum.

Intermediate goals can be thought of in terms of the task (task analysis) or of the teacher's role. The more usual way of thinking about planning intermediate goals is the former: analysing the task or activity. Both of these are linked with sustaining progression and continuity in children's learning and so building on success.

Analysing the task and the teacher's role

Teachers work, usually implicitly, with models of broad sequences of learning. These underlie their choices, in a 'child-centred' classroom, about provision for children's opportunities for learning or, in a more 'teacher-centred' environment, about which learning tasks are presented to children. How these kinds of models or 'images' develop has been the focus of work on the development of teachers' professional knowledge (for example, Elbaz 1983, Calderhead 1988).

It is important to work out what may be the components that are involved in acquiring a particular area of learning because, through these, the next steps in the child's learning can be identified. This is so whether the teacher supports a relatively child-centred or a subject-centred approach to fostering children's learning. In the former case, the identification of components or intermediate goals will lead the teacher to guide the child towards certain activities and to provide particular resources; in the latter case, teaching will be explicitly directed at the components (for example, Reason and Boote 1986, 1994; Solity and Bull 1987). Similarly, different theoretical stances in special education, including behavioural (for example, Ainscow and Tweddle 1979) and cognitive (Sugden 1989, Ashman and Conway 1989), advocate division of learning targets into possibly broad, but smaller, steps. This advocacy is continued in various National Curriculum documents. For example:

> In the process of giving pupils with s.e.n. the opportunity to demonstrate their level on the statements of attainment, teachers will often find it necessary to structure their schemes of work in such a way as to provide a series of intermediate goals, though it will be found that some attainment targets can be broken down more easily than others into smaller steps. In such circumstances teachers will want to adapt their existing record systems to bring them in line not only with the statements of attainment themselves but with the small steps leading to them.
>
> (National Curriculum Council 1989d: 12)

Teacher observations of the child (discussed in Chapter 4) will help the teacher to decide when, and in how much detail, activities need to be divided into smaller steps. The greater a child's difficulties in learning, the sharper will be the need for a focus on dividing activities into tentative 'intermediate goals'. The need, within the National Curriculum framework, to subdivide elements of the programmes of study into smaller parts, especially those relevant to key stage 1, is apparent from various research evidence.

Dylan Wiliam (1992) and his colleagues have shown that substantial minorities of each age group are unlikely to reach the original thresholds for the various key stages. For example, on the basis of pre-National Curriculum research into mathematical understanding, Dylan Wiliam has speculated that 9 per cent of

11-year-olds would fail to reach level 2 (the original lower boundary for work at key stage 2). Such studies indicate that there is a longer 'tail' to the spread in National Curriculum attainment targets than was originally envisaged. While the changes to the National Curriculum (SCAA 1994a, DFE 1995) make it permissible for children to work outside the range of work for their key stages, this does not alter the 'failure' attached to doing so.

A number of individuals, groups of teachers, and educationalists have produced possible divisions of the programmes of study relevant to children with learning difficulties (for example, Evans 1990, Tilstone and Steel 1989, Coventry LEA 1992). It has been argued that, in this way, the National Curriculum can be made to accommodate the learning needs of children with a wide range of difficulties, including children with multiple and profound learning difficulties. This approach works well for sequential and hierarchical skills, such as some aspects of number, and there is research support for the approach in that context (Cronbach and Snow 1977). However, attempts to produce definitive teaching or learning sequences for broader conceptual development have failed. Robert Gagné (1968), investigating this issue, emphasised the ability of a learner to skip sections, to draw on skills from other curricular or psychological areas, to use atypical combinations of sub-skills to arrive at a target and to achieve success by 'scrambled' sequences.

Planning programmes of study for children within level 1

At key stage 1, the planning of learning opportunities should take into account pre-infant school experiences. This planning may involve Health, Education and care services in the public as well as the voluntary sectors. It is vital that there is not only coordination across these services but also a direct link with the work of the reception class teacher.

It is more positive to use level 1 as a broad initial level within which all children can, at minimum, be seen to be working, than to regard children who fall below level 1 as 'off' the National Curriculum. Documentation about the National Curriculum has wavered between describing level 1 as meaning anything up to and including level 1 (i.e. level 1 as a broad phase) and level 1 as a specific 'benchmark' which children have not reached until they are able to complete a majority of the level 1 work (this is discussed further in Chapter 10).

A good starting point for the mainstream teacher of children with learning difficulties is to consider broadly a whole range of activities which might help a child to achieve early parts of the programmes of study.

English, attainment target 2: reading (level 1 – level description)

Pupils recognise familiar words in simple texts. They use their knowledge of letters and sound–symbol relationships in order to read words and to establish meaning when reading aloud. In these activities they sometimes require support. They express their response to poems, stories and non-fiction by identifying aspects they like.

(DFE 1995 English: 28)

The associated programme of study is directed at the whole of key stage 1 and so includes a broad range of suggested activities. These include children listening to sounds in oral language; listening to books, stories and poems; taking part in shared reading experiences with other children and the teacher; and retelling or re-reading familiar stories and poems. Children who need to use non-sighted methods of reading should be encouraged through appropriate methods of communication. The list below is the kind of thing that teacher groups, planning how parts of programmes of study might be subdivided, have evolved.

Programmes of study for children within level 1 on English attainment target 2 might include the following intermediate activities. These are not sequential or comprehensive:

- watching another child, or an adult, looking at a book;
- sharing a book with an adult;
- sharing a book with another child;
- choosing a book to look at from a classroom book area;
- hearing print in a familiar context, e.g. from a known story;
- hearing print in an unfamiliar context, e.g. from a birthday card;
- activities linking the written symbols with meaningful messages, e.g. counting from a written list of names the numbers of children having school dinner;
- collecting a variety of printed media (e.g. music scores, birthday cards, bottle labels) that convey information;

- 'reading' a book in role play (later recognising rules concerning the direction of print);
- letter/word games, e.g. finding the first letter of the child's name in other contexts (e.g. on road signs, in a teacher's name), at first with adult help then independently;
- decoding some basic sight vocabulary words from the daily environment (e.g. classroom, street, home);
- 'playing' with rhyming words;
- games involving recognising individual letter sounds in different contexts;
- games involving identifying individual letter sounds in different contexts;
- games involving recognising individual letter symbols in different contexts;
- games involving identifying individual letter symbols in different contexts;
- games involving matching individual letter sounds with their written symbols (and vice versa);
- retelling to an adult, with some prompting, incidents from (and later the main story-line) of a story, film or event;
- Retelling, without any adult prompting, a sequence of events;
- Inventing own stories stimulated by a variety of media (pictures, events, objects, dramatic play, etc.);
- Making own story and reading books using words/sentences written by an adult but dictated by the child (building up from single word to simple sentences, and beyond).

In a lively classroom many of the usual activities associated with, for example, a listening corner, work in the local environment and (for younger children) play in a home corner or (for older children) drama-based activities, are likely to promote acquisition of these components. If a child seems to be having great difficulty in one or more of these activities, it would be appropriate to plan a structured teaching programme to promote learning in relation to the learning goals of that activity. For example, a child who does not enjoy books might be involved in a series of activities associated with listening skills. For example:

- sharing music;
- watching brief videos of simple stories;
- handling books in various contexts (e.g. holding it for an adult to read);

- looking at pictures/photographs with an adult.

Other examples of possible activities of early parts of programmes of study for children within level 1 are described below. In all cases these are tentative and intended only as starting points for discussion and planning teaching. The suggested activities do not form comprehensive or prescriptive lists, nor do they represent linear teaching sequences. They would provide markers to indicate how a child's learning is progressing. There are further examples in *A Curriculum for All* (National Curriculum Council 1989d).

Science attainment target 1: experimental and investigative science (Level 1 – level description)

> Pupils describe simple features of objects, living things and events they observe, communicating their findings in simple ways, such as by talking about their work or through drawings or simple charts.
>
> (DFE 1995 Science: 50)

Possible activities in early parts of programmes of study include:

- discussion about materials collected by the child;
- discussion of adults' collections of objects based on a particular criterion (e.g. various foodstuffs all of which contain cinnamon);
- games, with adult guidance, involving identifying certain sounds as higher/lower in pitch/tone than other sounds;
- activities in which the child, prompted by an adult or friend, has to recognise certain tastes, scents, textures, pictures, having been told the identities of the items as a group (e.g. recognising, by their taste, sugar, lemon, curry);
- games in which the child has to recall, without any hints, tastes, scents, textures, pictures (e.g. recalling, by their scent, an orange, a highly perfumed flower, wood);
- paired discussion in which the child talks to a friend about an event;
- group discussion in which the child tells a group of classmates about an event;
- independent 'projects' involving describing (to another child) what is happening (e.g. watching two colours mixing);
- language games involving describing hidden objects to another child/group of children.

For a child who had difficulty in discussing groups of objects with an adult (the first two activities described above), additional activities such as the following might be developed:

- making collections of some sort;
- sharing a favourite object with an adult or another child.

Some of these activities could also be used as components of programmes of study towards other attainment targets; for example, music and English (attainment target 1, level 1 description).

Mathematics attainment target 4: handling data (Level 1 – level description) (This attainment target does not apply to key stage 1.)

> Pupils sort objects and classify them, demonstrating the criterion they have used.
>
> (DFE 1995 Mathematics: 29)

Possible activities in early parts of programmes of study for children within level 1 could include:

- sorting objects with adult guidance; for example, sorting cutlery into the various sets of implements;
- choosing sets containing more/less/the same number of objects;
- completing simple mapping diagrams using picture cards (e.g. story-book characters with appropriate object – fairy with wand, Father Christmas with sack of toys, a footballer with his team, a pop singer with his or her band), initially with adult help then independently;
- assembling a group of objects that belong together in some way (e.g. making a shell collection) and explaining the basis for the grouping;
- making a drawing of something seen around the school (e.g. a bird at a bird table);
- making drawings depicting things that go together (e.g. family and clothes at a festival or special event);
- playing games involving asking other children for more/less, same, . . . and for things belonging with others.

For a child with persistent difficulties in sorting objects with adult guidance (the first activity above), intermediate goals might encompass these activities, carried out with an adult:

- matching objects that are the same;
- matching pictures that are the same;
- matching by shape (2D and 3D);
- matching by colour;
- matching by similarity of touch or sound (progressivly moving from widely differing to less widely differing objects/pictures on the key criterion);
- matching objects that are different but have one key criterion in common (e.g. different types of doll of which two have the same colour dresses);
- identifying the odd one out in a group (increasing the number in the group and the magnitude of the difference).

For all of these, there should be a move from recognition to recall, for example, 'Find me the one that matches this' (recognition) to 'Can you find two that match?' (recall).

Subdividing programmes of study within key stages 1 and 2

The previous section has examined some ways of dividing early parts of programmes of study relating to level 1 of the level descriptions into possible component activities for children working within level 1. Not all children experiencing difficulties in learning in primary schools will still be at that stage. Many will be between (say) levels 1 and 2 of certain attainment targets. For example, a 9-year-old may be able to communicate meaning in writing through simple words and phrases (English, attainment target 3, level 1 description), but still be some way from writing in which ideas are developed in a sequence of sentences, sometimes demarcated by capital letters and full stops (level 2 description, DFE 1995 English: 30).

The teacher has to find a way of helping a child move between these two levels, perhaps taking the whole of key stages 1 and 2 to do so. The same kind of process as that described earlier of identifying a series of activities, this time spanning several levels of an attainment target, will be needed.

Subdividing parts of programmes of study is important because it will help the teacher to check that a child is making progress. Without such a subdivision a child may appear to be 'standing still' for long periods of time. Some examples of subdivisions of parts of programmes of study are given below.

English attainment target 3: level 2 – level description

Simple, monosyllabic, words are usually spelt correctly, and where there are inaccuracies the alternative is phonetically plausible.

(DFE 1995 English: 30)

For key stage 1, the associated programme of study includes the conventions of writing, writing single and joining letters, recognising and using simple spelling patterns, spelling words with common prefixes and suffixes, and the use of word books and dictionaries.

How might a teacher begin to plan the curriculum for a child (say an 8-year-old) who achieved level 1 in year 1 but has apparently had difficulty in extending his or her bank of correctly spelled monsyllabic words and uses random guesses not phonetically plausible alternatives (i.e. progressing to level 2)? An initial step would be to try to list the amount that the child could do, relevant to the level 1 and level 2 descriptions. For example, the child might be identified as attaining level 1 in English, attainment target 3 (writing) but have considerable gaps within this, such as poor letter formation, which is slowing progress to higher levels. This would involve making the kind of subdivision of the level 1 description discussed in the previous section. Having done this, the teacher could clarify the extent to which the child could achieve level 1. Teaching could then carry on from the appropriate point. It would be useful to check acquisition and fluency of the aspects identified (as discussed in Chapter 3). Perhaps progress to level 2 is slow because the child, although able to write single letter sounds and names, is very cautious about this (for any of several reasons, including hearing difficulties and lack of confidence).

Activities to develop English attainment target 3 in relation to the spelling strand (not a sequential or comprehensive list) could include:

- writing individual letters with adult guidance, given the letter sound as the cue;

- writing letters with adult guidance, given the letter name as the cue;
- recognising individual letter sounds and names;
- recalling individual letter sounds and names;
- reading letter sounds, within words (as appropriate) with adult guidance;
- matching individual letter shapes, with adult guidance;
- writing letters with adult prompting, given the letter sound as the cue;
- writing letters with adult prompting, given the letter name as the cue;
- finding words in a simple picture dictionary, having been helped to locate the first letter;
- writing words, given letter-by-letter sounding out by another child or by an adult;
- writing words, given letter-by-letter names by another child or by an adult;
- writing the first letter of words for classroom notices;
- recognising whether words come in the first or last half of the dictionary/word book;
- playing 'dictionary games' involving locating the correct page/ section for a word;
- independently finding words sought in simple picture dictionaries, then in dictionaries without illustrations;
- 'sounding out' words for other children;
- telling other children spellings using letter names;
- using a variety of dictionaries and word books to find spellings;
- using a variety of dictionaries and word books to find word meanings.

These activities would need to be part of a much wider, general English programme in the class so that the skills do not develop in isolation but within a context which gives them meaning.

At the start of this section, I referred to amount of adult help as being another way of thinking about planning intermediate goals. It will be evident that this dimension cross-references with the analysis of the activity, as outlined in the above examples. Although the two ways of breaking down tasks go side by side, it may be useful to bear the two distinct strategies in mind so that one or both are considered when children seem to find an activity difficult.

CONCLUSION

Planning intermediate goals is probably the most widely considered way of giving access to the National Curriculum to children who find learning difficult. It has the endorsement of the National Curriculum Council's special needs working party (National Curriculum Council 1989d) and has been taken up by practitioners. There are some points to bear in mind when planning intermediate goals:

- It is easier to apply this to some curricular areas than to others. Skills, in general, lend themselves to this approach whereas broader conceptual thinking does not.
- It is not possible to define categorically, in advance, 'correct' sequences of learning which will work for all children or even one specific child.
- Intermediate goals can be conceived in terms of amount and type of adult help as well as the nature of the activity.

Dividing programmes of study into intermediate goals is one strategy to use in order to give children with learning difficulties access to the National Curriculum. This can help to show that those children are making progress, even if this is in small steps, towards the same attainment targets as other children. It is important that broader approaches go alongside these small steps. Otherwise opportunities to apply and to generalise skills and knowledge may be lost. Some other ways of giving all children access to the National Curriculum are discussed in the next chapter.

Chapter 6

Differentiating teaching approaches

UNDERLYING PRINCIPLES

'Cold callers' trying to sell products often fail because they have only one way of presenting their materials. The more sophisticated, and successful, sales people have a range of techniques which they use depending on the circumstances and reactions of the potential purchaser. Similarly, in teaching, effective teachers adjust their style to individual learners. However, enthusiasm for differentiation needs to be constrained by realism. The discussion paper on curriculum organisation and classroom practice in primary schools recognised this:

> Given that significant progress could be made through a more efficient use of teaching time, we must add that the idea that at any one time learning tasks in nine subjects can be exactly matched to the needs and abilities of all the pupils in a class is hopelessly unrealistic. Match and differentiation are critical to effective learning, but they are aspirations rather than absolutes. In current circumstances the best the teacher can do (and it is a great deal) is to devise the classroom settings and pupil tasks which give the best chance of success.
>
> (Alexander *et al.* 1992: para. 110)

It is also worth remembering that undifferentiated work may have unexpected benefits, such as introducing an 'unready' child to a topic which unexpectedly seizes his or her imagination. It is important that a differentiated curriculum does not become an impoverished curriculum.

The reason for trying to differentiate the curriculum more effectively is to increase children's learning. Guidance from the

National Curriculum Council concerning children with special educational needs has contained some helpful examples of ways of differentiating particular tasks. (See National Curriculum Council 1992a, 1992b, 1992c.) Differentiation of teaching approaches encompasses a vast range of possibilities. These include differentiation according to: interests (working on a task through material of particular interest to the child), presentation of the activity (for example, this might be oral or written), response to the task (this could be oral, written or practical), grouping (children might work individually, in pairs, small groups, or as a whole class), pace (the same set of material as classmates but moving through it comparatively rapidly or slowly), sequence (task order varies, as in 'roundabout' systems in some primary classrooms) and support (with another child, a technological aid, a classroom helper or a support teacher) (Lewis 1992).

This chapter will focus on three main ways of differentiating teaching approaches: interest levels, presentation of activities and response to activities. These strategies are relevant to the implementation of the Code of Practice (DFE 1994a) as evidence collected about how teaching has been differentiated will show how the school has responded to individual learning needs. The following chapter looks at a broader aspect of differentiation: the grouping of children for learning.

FOCUSING ON TOPICS WHICH MATCH THE CHILD'S INTEREST LEVELS

Fitting interest levels of children with the demands of particular activities is one way in which some children can be given greater access to the National Curriculum. One approach, often advocated in early childhood education, is to develop child-initiated work, often around a cross-curricular topic (Bruce 1987). This has been advocated on the grounds that subsequent work is more likely to interest the child if the starting point has been self-selected by the child, rather than imposed by the teacher. This approach dovetails with the discussion of using topic work to help generalisation and adaptation of knowledge and skills (discussed in Chapter 3).

Parallel tasks: similar difficulty, different interests

In addition, specific parallel tasks can be planned so that, although the learning target is the same for a range of children, the means of promoting it reflect different interest levels. In a primary school, some 5-year-olds, 7-year-olds and 10-year-olds might all be at a similar level on specific attainment targets but it would not be appropriate to use the same type of learning materials with all three groups. Some teachers (at class, school and/or area levels) are developing banks of such parallel activities which are linked with parts of the National Curriculum. The materials, while different in focus and perhaps style, are all aimed at developing the same attainment targets. This is illustrated in the following examples of attainment targets and parts of their programmes of study. These are linked with activities which are relevant to children with varying interest levels.

Key stage 2, mathematics attainment target 4: handling data
(level 2 – level description)

> Pupils sort objects and classify them using more than one criterion. When they have gathered information, pupils record results in simple tables, block graphs and diagrams, in order to communicate their findings.
>
> (DFE 1995 Mathematics: 29)

The associated programme of study includes statements that children should interpret and create frequency tables, and should collect and represent discrete data appropriately.

Possible activities leading to these are, for a 7-year-old:

- graphing of months in which classmates have birthdays;
- using large, coloured, sticky squares to build up block graphs representing, for example, eye colour of children in the class;
- discussing similar charts compiled by other children or classes (e.g. shown in an assembly).

For a 9-year-old:

- making block graphs of types of vehicle passing the school (carried out in the course of a class project on transport), using 1 cm squared paper for recording;
- interviewing school personnel (e.g. about area in which holidays were taken) and compiling a block graph from this information;
- working in a team of children who have carried out this type of activity on related topics (e.g. method of transport used to reach

holiday destination, number of people in the holiday party), and discussing links across the block graphs (e.g. noticing any inconsistencies, such as if most people holiday in Cornwall and most people travel by air, there is probably something wrong with the graphs).

For an 11-year-old:

- collating information from classmates about their chosen secondary schools, using a microcomputer to build up the database and print out the block graph;
- listing numbers of goals scored by various footballers and presenting this information in several ways, including block graphs;
- using this as a basis for discussion with classmates about which players they would transfer/sell if they were the manager.

It is useful to think of a variety of contexts in which particular skills and knowledge could be developed, otherwise a child with difficulties in learning might experience, at different ages, very similar activities to promote particular attainment targets. Awareness of this problem has led to the development of teenage reading books with relatively low reading ages but with contents which are appropriate for a young person. Arguably, it is even more important to get the interest level right than it is to match the learning demands of the task with the child's capabilities. If the interest level is appropriate then the child may be sufficiently motivated to struggle through material which is too difficult.

This section has considered varying the context through which a task is developed by trying to match the interest level of the child with the focus of the task. The following sections discuss varying the ways in which, first, an activity is presented to a child and, second, a child might respond.

VARYING THE PRESENTATION OF THE ACTIVITY

A group of children may be working together on, say, making a weather station. The teacher could allow for children of different abilities within the group by varying the level of questions that he or she asks and by presenting the activities in different ways to children, depending on what is appropriate for individuals.

Teachers' questions/comments

Many teachers vary the level of talk, especially questions, directed to different children in ways which are intuitively tuned in to the varying ability levels of the children. This is one way of differentiating the task so that it is adjusted for different children. However, research on teachers' talk in classrooms (e.g. Wood *et al.* 1980, Tizard and Hughes 1984, Edwards and Westgate 1987, Wells 1987) suggests that teachers' talk is often not well attuned to individual children. In particular, it tends to be pitched too low in terms of linguistic and cognitive demands. This is no doubt related in part to the heavy managerial demands of the classroom. Teachers spend much of the time organising the class as a whole and have only brief exchanges with individual children. The National Curriculum is helping to focus attention on to the quality of teaching exchanges and to encourage more careful matching of teachers' questions with children's cognitive levels. Many of the points raised in Chapter 4 about an adult's talk in child–adult conferences apply here also.

Presentation of activities

Another way of differentiating the task input so that it is matched to individual children is to use a range of media (tapes, microcomputers, workcards and task sheets, etc.) through which the child accesses the task. Thus, if children are, for example, relatively poor at reading, they may listen to instructions (from a tape or from another child) and so continue the activity. They are not prevented from following an activity just because, at the outset, they cannot gain access to it. This could be particularly important, if all classroom activities are mediated through English, for children for whom English is their second language.

The programmes of study make explicit reference to the need to make appropriate provision for children to use augmented communication (for example, signing, Braille, or lip reading), technological aids and aids to allow access to practical activities within and beyond school. What sort of help is available and what range of things might this differentiation of access involve? NCET material (1994b) outlines ways in which microcomputers may help to provide access to activities. Examples of provision for children with learning difficulties include joystick, keyguard, overlay keyboard, printer, speech synthesiser, switches, tracker-ball, touch screen, integral mouse/mat pad, mouse drivers enabling cursor size, shape and colour to be modified, and a variable height trolley. This NCET publication also contains a useful checklist to help teachers examine the context of a child's learning and to evaluate appropriate technological provision. Key questions relate to:

- context (e.g. what has been tried in the past? why change now?);
- purpose (e.g. what is the technology intended to achieve?);
- continuity (e.g. is the child familiar with information technology?);
- support (e.g. have the child's parents been involved in discussions about the equipment?);
- management (e.g. have security, insurance and maintenance been considered?);
- monitoring (e.g. what criteria will be used to monitor the learning objectives?);
- transition (e.g. what planning is in place for considering the changing needs of the child?).

Parallel questions could be applied to any of the strategies or resources, mentioned earlier, for increasing children's access to activities.

Modifying written presentations of tasks

Many activities in primary classrooms start from written instructions on workcards, task sheets, a classroom notice or in workbooks. Before considering ways of modifying the presentation of such written task sheets, the purpose of the activity should be considered. HMI found that worksheets were often little more than word or gap-filling exercises. Similarly, worksheets may require much colouring in of shapes or pictures and be effective ways of keeping children occupied but do little to promote or consolidate understanding and knowledge. The former may occasionally be justified but not under the guise of the latter.

Routine written material in classrooms may require surprisingly high reading levels. An interesting study examined the readability levels of textual material found in schools from year 2 to year 10 (Sawyer et al. 1994). The reading levels required to read a sample of textbooks, workcards and worksheets were calculated. In all the years surveyed a significant amount of classroom reading material was found to be too difficult for the vast majority of pupils in that year. Humanities and science materials were particularly difficult. This suggests that children with reading difficulties are likely to be particularly hampered in these subjects unless materials are modified for them, they work with more able classmates and/or the teacher goes through materials in detail with these children. Chris Sawyer and his colleagues note that it would help teachers to gauge the appropriateness of reading materials if publishers included specific readability information with those materials.

Much work has been carried out at secondary school level to modify worksheets, workcards and textbooks (referred to collectively here as 'written task sheets') for children with learning difficulties. Modifications have centred on reducing reading level without reducing content. There are relevant implications for planning written task sheets at key stages 1 and 2. Robin Lloyd-Jones (1985), Peter Croft (1989), Desmond McAsey (n.d.) and others have produced comprehensive advice about designing written task sheets for children who have difficulties in learning. The following checklist provides a guide to making or evaluating written task sheets:

Approach

- use material that is within, or close to, the child's experience;
- introduce new concepts in familiar contexts or settings;
- make the tasks self-contained;
- provide plenty of clues, cues and examples;
- give plenty of opportunities for success;
- make sure that the illustrations tie in closely with the text;
- use active rather than passive verbs;
- use pupils' contributions (e.g. a logo);
- use pupils' feedback to decide whether or not the written task sheets fulfil your educational aims and objectives;
- supplement with a taped version of the task sheet;
- if possible, try out several versions of a written task sheet,

Presentation

- differentiate clearly between text and instructions;
- leave a wide border all round the edge of the page;
- highlight and explain new words;

- use type/print not handwriting;
- use a print size compatible with the size of the children's handwriting;
- use sub-headings to structure the written task sheet;
- check that there are no more than ten words in each line for upper primary children and fewer than this for younger children;
- use a simple, uncluttered layout;
- break up continuous blocks of text;
- consider using a desk top publishing program to produce materials which look attractive, are effective and can be readily modified;
- use illustrations;
- highlight instructions in some way (e.g. boxed);
- use coloured as well as white paper (both for variety and for coding purposes, e.g. extension material on yellow paper) but be careful not to use certain combinations of ink and paper (e.g. red/orange with green/brown) as these may cause problems for children who are colour blind.

Language

- use short sentences and simple sentence structure;
- avoid ambiguous words.

Problems of ambiguity in verbal instructions were discussed in Chapter 4 in relation to child–adult conferences. Similar problems may be present in written material. The two workcards in Figures 6.1 and 6.2 contain unintentional ambiguity, resulting in confusion and 'errors' for children who followed them literally.

How many litle jugs fit into the big jug?

Figure 6.1 Workcard for water play during work on capacity (children were given several jugs of different sizes, one jug of each size)

> **Put the worm on a piece of paper.**
>
> **Put a dot at each end of the worm.**
>
> **Measure how long the worm is.**

Figure 6.2 Workcard for a project on worms

VARYING CHILDREN'S MODES OF RESPONSE

Another strategy which may be used to help children with learning difficulties to participate in National Curriculum programmes of study is to examine different ways in which a child might develop and demonstrate abilities in particular programmes of study. Surveys of primary education (for example, Alexander *et al.* 1992, OFSTED 1993b) have found an over-reliance on writing as the vehicle for demonstrating and consolidating learning. An over-reliance on children's written responses can easily lead to an underestimation of the knowledge and skills possessed by children with learning difficulties. In turn, this underestimation is likely to lead to teaching which is aimed at too low a level for the child. Changing the mode of response to be used will not usually change the focus of the learning. To say '2 added to 2 makes 4' is as correct as writing '2+2=4' if it is the numerical knowledge which the teacher wants the child to demonstrate. Only a small minority of attainment targets specify that a particular type of response is required. For example, where handwriting is a specific target then children whose disability is such that handwriting is impossible will need to be exempted from those aspects of the programmes of study. Such children could follow other aspects of the writing programmes of study as these encourage the use of technological aids.

The East Sussex special needs advisory team has produced materials about differentiation which include ideas for varying children's ways of responding to a task (Elliott *et al.* 1992). These ideas include varying the type of written task, using not just conventional accounts but also letters, crosswords, maps and plans, diaries, instructions, drama scripts, leaflets, poems, advertisements, newspapers, charts and graphs. Suggestions for various pictorial responses include posters, cartoons, collages, displays and models. Oral responses might involve video or audio recordings, debates, inquiries, trials, drama and role play, individual, pair or group presentations. Given this wide range of possibilities it seems rather unimaginative to end a project or activity with the bland instruction to 'Write what you have found out about. . .'.

Children with difficulties in learning may have problems with reading and writing but may be very competent in practical tasks. Science and design and technology programmes of study may, in particular, lend themselves to being developed orally and practically for children with learning difficulties, although classmates may use written methods. Some history and geography attainment targets could be developed through role play. Science, design and technology, and mathematics could be fostered through the child manipulating concrete materials and showing/describing the result to an adult rather than writing down the findings. This stance is supported by the findings of a survey by HMI of children with special needs in mainstream schools. This survey noted: 'Work of at least satisfactory quality was often associated with experience-based learning activities which used a range of media and practical activities' (DES 1989a: para. 15).

This point is illustrated by examining some extracts from programmes of study. In science, at key stage 2, children should be taught to carry out fair tests (DFE 1995). Children with poor reading levels may have difficulty in demonstrating this if the work requires reading instructions from a book or workcard and writing the answer. This does not mean that the child is unable to make the scientific judgements but that he or she is prevented from showing this because the means of communication is based on a weakness, for the child, not a strength. If, instead, work towards this part of the programme of study involves the child in a large amount of firsthand experience, including discussion of results with classmates, then such scientific understanding might well be demonstrated.

Children who find school-based learning difficult may need to manipulate concrete materials in order to understand the basic concepts. Although this is a regular part of early learning it may be more difficult to find ways of introducing concrete materials into activities with older children, particularly if the materials are perceived as 'babyish'. Anne Henderson (1989) has described the sets of concrete materials which she made to help children to grasp concepts about place value. She made blocks to represent not just hundreds, tens and units (as in Dienes apparatus) but also three-dimensional 'decimal points' and blocks to represent one-tenth and one-hundredth. She gives an interesting account of games which she devised using these concrete materials. She believes that they were highly effective in developing both mathematical under-standing and self-confidence about maths. Similar approaches can be developed in other aspects of the curriculum.

Varying children's mode of response in topic work

Many primary schools use topic- or project-based approaches, within or across curricular areas, and these can be planned so that there are parallel activities in which children with learning difficulties participate alongside classmates. The trend seems to be towards topics which are closely, although not exclusively, subject based. Gone are the days of the vast topic web in which anything and everything which could conceivably be linked to some key theme was included in the project. One impact of the National Curriculum is the demise of the multi-subject topic. This was signalled in Eric Bolton's statement in his annual report: 'The weakest work in primary school occurs when too many aspects of different subjects are roped together within integrated themes or topic work' (DES 1990c: para. 36). The move away from multi-subject topics is reflected also in the use of HMI's areas of learning and experience as the basis for curriculum planning (discussed in Chapter 3)

Some possible parallel activities are outlined below for two typical primary school projects: 'Growth' and 'Shops'. (A similar approach is described more fully, in relation to a topic on 'Shipwreck', in Lewis and Thorpe 1989.) These parallel activities reflect flexibility and diversity in both possible presentation of activities and/or children's type of response.

Topic: growth

This is a science-based topic but also involves mathematics, English, design and technology and art. Possible activities include:

- Children could plant various things and monitor how they grow. Children with difficulties in learning could be encouraged to record observations by telling another child and/or by speaking into a tape recorder or *Language Master* machine, rather than necessarily making written recordings of observations. These could be developed as part of role playing the various parts of scientist, reporter, scribe, etc.
- Observational drawings could be made by all children. Children with difficulties could begin by making representational paintings rather than more precise drawings.
- All children could make paintings of impressions of, for example, woods, meadowland or grass, aiming to capture the 'feel' of the environment rather than actuality. (Music such as Vivaldi's *Four Seasons* could be used as a stimulus.)
- All children could look for relevant non-fiction books. If necessary, children with reading difficulties could share these with a competent child or adult in order to discover information.
- All children, but particularly those with learning difficulties, could use microcomputer-based simulation programs to develop ideas about plant requirements.
- Computer databases could be built up by the children collectively and used in various ways depending on children's mathematical skills and knowledge.
- Children could work in pairs of similar ability to devise apparatus to monitor aspects of plant growth. One pair of children might appropriately monitor rate of growth, devising a simple stand with horizontal scale; another pair might plan to monitor plant respiration. In this way children of widely varying attainments could be included in parallel activities and make complementary contributions to overall conclusions.
- Children could invent and model, or draw, their own versions of 'useful' plants, such as, a plant to collect wasps or, much more complex, a plant which could survive in an atmosphere with limited oxygen.
- A group or class book on growing things could contain contributions from a range of children. Children with learning difficulties could do illustrations: they could find, cut out from magazines and paste in relevant photographs, or make print pictures using various seeds, bulbs or leaves. They could write short contributions including, for example, a contents page and parts of a glossary. Word processors and desktop printing

packages could be used as well as, or instead of, handwritten material.

- Children could make collections of folk and fairy tales which are related to growing things. Some children could find these by reading a range of fiction. Children without sufficient reading abilities could interview adults and children (inside and outside the class) to make an oral collection of such stories.
- Whole class discussion about differences in rates of growth could include reflections about visual and sensory impairments. This could help children to recognise the continuum of normality.

Topic: shops

This is a geography/history-based topic but also involves English, mathematics, art and technology. Possible activities include:

- Children could use photographs, taken over a period of time, as the foci of discussion about changes in the area. Similarly, artefacts could stimulate discussion, conjecture and problem-solving among children with a range of attainments. Some children could compose 'headlines' for the photographs while other children write accompanying stories, depending on levels of interest, skill and motivation.
- Children could write accounts of what the shops used to be like. (If they are a recent development, the accounts might be about the area prior to the shops being built.) Children with difficulties in writing could dictate their accounts to an adult for writing, record their accounts on a tape recorder, or record changes pictorially through drawings or collections of news photographs.
- Children could role play various occupations associated with the running of a shop. Children could be divided into groups so that complexity of role is appropriate for the child. Relatively simple roles might include sales person, purchaser, delivery driver or cash till operator. More complex roles could include accountant, buyer, store detective, tax inspector, general manager, personnel officer, so that the topic is demanding of able children in the group or class as well as being appropriate for less able children.
- Role play and drama could include various purchasing simulations. Whether or not coins are available and the type of coins

used will depend on the children's levels. Some children might use, say, 5p, 10p and 20p coins while other children, in separate but parallel activities, might use the whole range of coins and notes. Yet other children might carry out transactions using 'cheques' (e.g. with the sales person mentally totalling the cost of goods and the purchaser writing out the 'cheque').

- A favourite shop could be selected and the source traced of chosen items. This would involve use of reference material and/or interviews with shopkeepers. Children with learning difficulties might do more of the oral work and fewer written activities than other children.
- Observational drawings could be made of the shops (interiors and/or exteriors) and associated people, with children using media (e.g. paint, wax crayon, pastel crayon, chalk, charcoal, drawing pencil, 'paint' software) appropriate to their abilities and experiences.
- Working models could be designed of, for example, trolleys to transport goods from delivery areas to shelves, conveyor belts to move goods across the checkout, and children's own inventions such as a machine to shop in a supermarket on behalf of an elderly person. Children with difficulties could be encouraged to develop relatively simple models (e.g. a shopping trolley or cart) while children with a good understanding of mechanical things could try to develop more complex models such as a robot shopper.
- Children could interview various adults working in the shops, in order to develop both ideas about the various roles and knowledge of the background to products. If children were to prepare the interview questions beforehand then all children could be involved in asking the questions. In mixed ability groups more able children could construct appropriate record sheets and summary forms.
- Children could invent orally, read and/or write a range of stories associated with shops. These might be relatively factual (e.g. accounts of a day in the life of a shop worker) or based on fantasy (e.g. a shop with a magic doormat). These kinds of activity could be carried out by all children at their own levels.
- Maps could be made to show the location of the shops. The sophistication of these would vary with children's abilities and understanding. Children with difficulties could be encouraged to begin by laying acetate sheets over aerial photographs and

drawing over the route, thus helping them to develop an understanding that maps represent real features.

- Accounts of changes in the shops could be written by children with learning difficulties by using successive cartoon-style boxes, with limited writing.
- Children could invent board games showing change in the area (e.g. one square represents ten years). Children of all abilities could contribute to this type of activity.
- Coins from different countries could be collected and analysed, divided into different sets on the basis of one, two or three criteria (e.g. size, shape, age, continent). This could lead to observational drawing. Both types of activity could be done at various levels of ability.
- The whole class could discuss adaptions in shops which would aid people with disabilities.

Many of these suggestions involve, as found in numerous primary schools, a strong emphasis on firsthand experience and oral means of communication. Varying the mode of chidren's responses, as described in these examples, may apply also to assessments of learning.

Examples

The final part of this chapter brings together the strategies described here and the planning of intermediate goals, discussed in Chapter 5, by describing two case studies showing ways in which the teacher might help children with difficulties in learning to gain access to specific aspects of the National Curriculum.

An example: Melvin

Melvin is 9 years old but his reading is at the level of an average 6/7-year-old. Other school attainments are, like his reading, 'behind' that of his peers. He has no special hobbies or interests but is enthusiastic about *Power Rangers*.

Action:

Melvin's class teacher has been using the *Ginn 360* reading scheme with Melvin but he has made little progress. The class teacher feels that this may be because he associates these books with his unsuccessful attempts to read. She has tried the *Breakthrough* materials but he is not enthusiatic about these because he says that they are 'babyish'.

The teacher decides to concentrate on one curricular area with Melvin. His main difficulties are in reading and this hampers other learning so, although his writing is also poor, she decides to focus on reading. She identifies Melvin as being past level 1 and near to level 2 in reading. He can read many of the signs and notices in the classroom, has some understanding of alphabetical order, uses picture but not context cues in his reading and has a very poor recall of events in a story although he seems to enjoy hearing stories. The range of reading material which he can and will read unprompted is very limited. He uses first letter cues to decode words but rarely uses other strategies. After this assessment the teacher decides to concentrate on developing Melvin's enjoyment, and recall, of stories.

Breaking down the task

The teacher identifies a series of activities which she hopes will develop Melvin's enjoyment and recall of stories. These activities, recorded on teaching plans and later on record sheets, are:

- watching a video of a short story (the topic chosen by Melvin);
- drawing a picture of one event from the story;
- re-telling to a friend or adult what is happening in the picture;
- responding to questions about what led up to and/or followed from the event depicted;
- placing in sequence a series of pictures about the taped story (if the story is seen or heard by some of the other children in the class then the pictures could be supplied by them or, if the story tape is commercially available, published sets of pictures might be available);
- re-enacting with friend(s) the events in the story;
- drawing a series of cartoon-style pictures to record key events in the story in sequence, starting with a series of three boxes and gradually increasing the number of boxes;
- writing, with a friend and perhaps using a word processor, an account of the story but with one or two key events changed;
- partnering a younger or less able child to whom he tells this story.

The teacher plans to use several different stories if Melvin becomes bored with the first story.

Matching interest level

If Melvin chooses the story, perhaps bringing in a video from home of a favourite story or series, then the activity is likely to be motivating for him because the interest level of the story/stories will be appropriate.

Alternative ways of presenting the task

The activities outlined above involve a variety of ways of presenting the task. None of them involves reading at this stage although this could be added when Melvin has completed the activities successfully.

Alternative modes of responding

The activities outlined above involve a variety of responses from Melvin but relatively little writing, which is one of his weak areas. Writing will be the focus of a separate teaching plan.

An example: Amanda

Amanda is an 8-year-old who is, in general, at level 2 on most level descriptions in the core subjects. Her general knowledge is quite good compared with peers but she has difficulty in various activities which involve spatial awareness and understanding. For example, she is often confused about her right- and her left-hand sides, she makes mistakes when trying to follow directions involving right and left, she confuses compass directions and finds drawing simple maps difficult. Amanda's care-givers have reported that she has had these types of difficulties for some time. Her favourite activity at home is playing with a puppet theatre made by an uncle.

The teacher is planning a topic related to the local environment. This will include drawing maps of the local area (Geography, programme of study for key stage 1) and the teacher anticipates that Amanda will find it difficult to complete some of the activities.

None of the children has worked extensively on this topic before as it is not in the school's scheme of work until year 3.

Action

Amanda's class teacher organises a discussion and preliminary activities with the whole class to assess how much they know in relation to this attainment target. She finds that Amanda can fulfil the level 1 description (for example, she recognises some specific places and geographical features) but cannot, as can other children who meet the level 2 description, use a map competently.

Breaking down the task

The teacher plans the following activities:

- recognising objects from their silhouettes (e.g. using shadows thrown up by an overhead projector);
- recognising objects on an outline plan;
- drawing several non-overlapping objects in outline;
- recognising overlapping objects on an outline plan;
- making a 3D-model of something in a picture or photograph;
- drawing front/rear views of a 3D object;
- tracing a picture (i.e. a 'front' view);
- drawing an aerial view of a 3D object;

Matching interest level

As Amanda is very interested in and enthusiastic about puppets, her teacher could use this interest to develop Amanda's mapping skills. Amanda could make a small puppet theatre from junk materials as part of craft activities and then various aspects of plan making could be carried out using the puppet theatre as the focus. This could involve, for example, drawing the puppet theatre as it appears to her looking down from above, as it appears to friends watching from the front and as it appears to someone watching from behind the puppet theatre. The puppet theatre activities could include shadow as well as 3D puppets and so help to develop Amanda's linking of 2D and 3D objects. She could go on to write plays for the puppets and these could involve directions about where the puppets have to move to and from. A range of 'director's materials' could show the plan of the stage, movements, etc.

Alternative ways of presenting the task/alternative modes of responding

The various puppet-play activities involve a wide range of ways of presenting of the task and types of response from Amanda. Written plans are drawn only at a relatively late stage.

CONCLUSION

Chapters 2 to 6 have looked at planning teaching and how, specifically, this planning can help children with difficulties in learning to have access to the National Curriculum and a broader curriculum beyond that. The next chapter moves the focus to the grouping of children in the classroom.

Chapter 7

Grouping

The basis on which children might be divided into teaching groups is an aspect of the National Curriculum that aroused controversy in relation to children with difficulties in learning. The first part of this chapter will review and evaluate what has been suggested regarding this topic in National Curriculum statutory and advisory documents. The second part focuses on implications for practice, including a particular aspect of the grouping of children: the integration of children from special schools and units into mainstream settings.

The National Curriculum lays down a framework of what should be taught at various stages and how this should be assessed but does not state the way in which it should be taught. In this respect the UK national curricula are less rigid than the national curricula which have been developed in some other countries. These, by stipulating some aspects of teaching method, such as the pacing of work and teaching materials, are more prescriptive.

Teaching method encompasses the approach to curriculum planning (for example, single-subject based, cross-curricular or a mixture of these), teaching materials (for example, reading schemes, 'real' books, mathematics equipment, materials for science experiments) and how the class is organised (for example, integrated day, mixed or single-ability groups). Commentaries and advice about teaching method and the National Curriculum have focused mainly on the first two of these three aspects. Several local education authorities and primary school interest groups have produced guidelines on planning topic work in the National Curriculum and published schemes which aim to teach successive levels of individual National Curriculum subjects. Relatively little discussion has taken place about classroom organisation, and specifically the grouping of children, in relation to teaching the National Curriculum.

RECOMMENDATIONS IN NATIONAL CURRICULUM DOCUMENTS CONCERNING GROUPING OF CHILDREN FOR TEACHING

There are two issues about the grouping of children for teaching that arise from National Curriculum documentation. One issue concerns the delimiting of levels and corresponding key stages. Revisions to the National Curriculum (SCAA 1994a, DFE 1995) have loosened the links between key stages and levels so that it is now permissible to teach outside the thresholds and ceilings for particular key stages. The main relevance of this for primary age children with special needs is that at key stage 2 (i.e. ages 7 to 11) children who are at level 1 can be taught level 1 material without this requiring formal modification or a statement. Similarly, very able children at key stages 1 or 2 can be taught material beyond the notionally designated levels for their key stages.

The second issue concerns how children are grouped for teaching. This falls outside the National Curriculum, as it is a matter of teaching method not curriculum content. Teaching method, as successive Secretaries of State for Education reiterated, is a matter for individual schools, rather than central government, to decide. This point was made again in the report on the 1994 consultation exercise:

> What should be taught is statutorily defined; how it is taught should be decided by individual schools . . . Such decisions are the proper exercise of teachers' professional judgements.
>
> (SCAA 1994a: 7)

Nevertheless, the Department of Education and Science (now the Department for Education) commented on pupil grouping and supported a mix of age and ability grouping. This contrasted with advice from the National Curriculum Council, which was more cautious about advocating ability grouping. Discussion of grouping by the level description reached led to questions about children repeating a year (a system termed *redoublement* in France and 'grade retention' in the United States).

Grouping of children into teaching groups

Whole class grouping by National Curriculum level

The National Curriculum structure of hierarchies of eight levels (plus an exceptional performance level) might be interpreted as encouraging the use of National Curriculum levels as the bases for teaching groups. Associated continuous teacher assessments will identify children as being, broadly, at one of eight levels in any particular subject. As each level in the National Curriculum was envisaged as representing two years of age, classes based on levels could still contain a wide range of attainment (DES/WO 1988). Consequently, considerable differentiation of work within the class would still be necessary (see Chapters 5 and 6). However, the range of attainments would be likely to be less wide than that found previously in most primary classes. The Cockcroft Report (DES 1982b) referred to a typical spread of attainments of seven years in classes of 11-year-olds (i.e. year 6).

There are difficulties associated with treating levels as the basis for allocating children to classes. (Their use in relation to 'setting' children within or across classes is considered below.) The first set of difficulties concerns determining a National Curriculum-based attainment level for a child. All of the child's attainments would have to be reduced to some single figure in order to decide which class a child should join. For example, if classes were based on single National Curriculum levels, how would a place in a (say) level 3 class be determined? Would this relate to only the core subjects? And what if attainment levels in the core subjects varied? It might be argued that a child in a level 3 class would have a majority of attainments at level 3, but some attainments might be seen as more central than others. Would allocation to classes be determined by, say, level on English targets because these might be said to underlie all other attainments? If this were the case it would disadvantage children for whom English is a second language. Would children be moved around mid-year to make adjustments for those who had, for example, already progressed to level 4?

Even if these kinds of argument could be resolved satisfactorily, one is attributing a spurious accuracy to National Curriculum levels by using them as the basis for placement. The levels are not precise, nor is their validity based on systematic research evidence.

The specifications of levels in the revised attainment targets remain best guesses, although they are the result of modification through teachers' experience of the National Curriculum.

The second set of difficulties concerning streaming children on the basis of National Curriculum levels relates to children's wider development. If there is a 'level 2' class in a primary school then, in theory, this might contain a majority of 7-year-olds plus some younger children with relatively high attainments for their ages and some older children with relatively low attainments for their ages. The chronological spread might easily range from 5-year-olds to 9-year-olds. A child with learning difficulties might remain at one level for a relatively long time (perhaps four or five years compared with two years for peers). A child with severe learning difficulties who is integrated into a mainstream primary school operating this system could, theoretically, end up spending almost all of his or her school career in a level 1 class while successive groups of peers ripple past him or her. There could be enormous developmental differences between, for example, able 5-year-olds, 'average' 7-year-olds and 9-year-olds with learning difficulties, in spite of similarities in attainment terms. To group these children together for teaching makes sense only if academic development is the sole consideration. If personal and social development are also to be fostered then class grouping on the basis of similarities in curricular attainments becomes of questionable value.

The National Curriculum Council was cautious about streaming, stating that children with or without statements may be in a teaching group of younger pupils but that: 'It is the view of National Curriculum Council that this option will not often be practicable or educationally desirable and will be kept under review' (National Curriculum Council 1989d: 10). Martin Davies, then Director of the National Curriculum Council, reinforced this stance: 'There is no need for remedial classes and there is no need for pupils to be taught in groups of a different age . . . we don't want the dynamic to move in the direction of level 1 remedial groups' (National Curriculum Council 1989e: 3). On similar lines, HMI, in their review of children with statements in ordinary schools (DES 1990d) were more positive about grouping these children with other mainstream pupils on the basis of chronological age rather than by attainment. More recently, SCAA and the DFE have made little comment about pupil grouping in relation to the National Curriculum.

Streaming is likely to be detrimental for children with learning difficulties. A consistent finding in research into streaming is that it tends to diminish the self-esteem of children in 'lower' streams. In an extensive review of the effects of streaming on cognitive aspects of development (Cronbach and Snow 1977), it is emphasised that dividing children into streams and teaching them separately can only be justified if this separation can be shown to be more effective than when the children are taught together. The authors conclude that the research evidence is equivocal and does not support streaming as a means of improving academic learning for the whole ability range. Robert Slavin (1987) has made a similar, detailed analysis of research into grouping and children's attainments in elementary schools. He reviewed a large number of American studies which monitored the effects of three types of grouping: streaming, setting across classes and within-class attainment grouping. He concluded that:

- pupils should be based in mixed attainment classes for most of the time;
- grouping should reduce heterogeneity in the specific subject being taught (e.g. reading) not in broad terms (e.g. general ability);
- grouping plans should be flexible and so open to revision;
- the number of groups formed within-classes should be kept small so that the teacher can adjust teaching appropriately to the different groups.

Both these reviews focused on American research. However, it is likely that the findings are applicable to the British context.

The possibility of redoublement

In theory, the concept of *redoublement* cannot be applied to the operation of the National Curriculum because the National Curriculum contains no notion of absolute pass and fail. Children are judged against several series of curriculum-based assessments. However, the levels are being interpreted by some schools and local education authorities as precise and normative. This has opened the way for the argument that some children will 'fail' to meet a norm (for example, level 4 at age 11) and so will need to retake earlier work. Wandsworth advocated streaming on the basis of children's National Curriculum levels and extended this, saying that children would have to retake a year if they did not reach satisfactory levels.

The Department of Education and Science did not advocate making children who 'fail' a year repeat the year. However, the point was phrased negatively and weakly: 'There is nothing in the 1988 or 1993 Education Acts to require pupils to repeat a year, nor to prevent an early move to another year group' (Circular 15/89, DES 1989g: para. 33). The tone of Circular 15/89 was strengthened in a later circular (3/90) in which a similar statement to that given above was followed by: *'except where the school judges this to be in the best interests of the pupil'* (DES 1990e: para. 23 ii; emphasis added). Such a justification could be applied very widely and could be defended, by a determined local education authority or school, on so many different grounds that opponents would have a hard time defeating such justifications.

The emphasis should be on finding appropriate teaching approaches rather than assuming that children who 'fail' to meet certain criteria need merely to repeat methods which have been demonstrably unsuccessful. This point is supported by the findings of American research into grade retention. One American study found that, annually, between 5 and 7 per cent of children in state ('public') schools in the US repeated a grade (Shepard and Smith 1990). A surprisingly large number of children were affected. These researchers suggested that 'by 9th grade approximately half of all US school students have flunked at least one grade (or are no longer in school)' (Shepard and Smith 1990: 84). This report reviewed evidence about the effects of grade retention and concluded:

> Contrary to popular belief repeating a grade actually worsens achievement levels in subsequent years . . . There are numerous ways to provide extra instructional help focused on a student's specific learning needs within the context of normal grade promotion. Remedial help, before and after school programs, summer school, instructional aides to work with target children in the regular classroom, and no-cost peer tutoring are all more effective than retention.
>
> (Shepard and Smith 1990: 85)

Setting and within-class grouping of children

The Department of Education and Science seemed to be moving towards advocating setting, and sometimes streaming, of pupils.

Circular 5/89 (issued in February 1989) referred to the possibility that:

> An individual pupil might, however, be younger or older [than the majority of pupils in a class or teaching group]. . . This enables a pupil to be taught with another age group for *one or more* subject areas where appropriate.
>
> (DES 1989b: para. 33; emphasis added)

More strongly, *From Policy to Practice*, issued May 1989, stated:

> Individual pupils can, as some do now, work with a class of older or younger pupils, for some or *all* subjects.
>
> (DES 1989f: para. 8.2; emphasis added)

The document, *A Framework for the Primary Curriculum* (National Curriculum Council 1989c), considered the issue of grouping of pupils and reviewed the varieties and purposes of different forms of grouping. It did not favour any specific form of grouping and concluded:

> The clarity of the National Curriculum subject requirements and detailed information about pupils' achievements will allow teachers to ensure grouping arrangements are made appropriately. At all times, the needs of the individual pupil should be given the highest priority.
>
> (National Curriculum Council 1989c: 11)

The emphasis here was on using different forms of grouping as appropriate and that 'there may be occasions' on which it is appropriate for able children to work with older children. This stance accords well with evidence from various research (for example, Galton *et al.* 1980, Bennett 1990, Hastings and Schwieso 1995) which has advocated flexibility in classroom groupings and a mix of individual, small-group and whole-class work. The National Curriculum Council's advisory document on the National Curriculum and special needs (National Curriculum Council 1989d) also stated that good learning environments will be characterised by flexible groupings. Robin Alexander and his co-authors (1992) discussed this issue and concluded 'The critical notion is that of fitness for purpose' (1992: para. 101). There is a place for whole-class teaching as well as working in small groups. It makes sense to group children in small groups when they are intended to work closely together. If children are responding to a whole class lesson then it is likely to be more effective if seating arrangements reflect this. However, realistically, time will probably be wasted if there is constant switching from one arrangement to another. Classroom layouts need to be planned to reflect the dominant teaching style with as much flexibility as is feasible and appropriate.

Mixed-ability classes with some setting into work groups of children at similar levels of attainment within the class or across several classes would avoid many of the difficulties associated with allocating children to fixed-class groups according to National Curriculum level. However, the need to be tentative about levels still applies if these are used as the basis for planning work groups within the class. It is easier to retain this tentativeness if groupings are flexible. Apparent anomalies (e.g. 'This child comes out at level 3 in maths but there are still some level 2 activities which he needs to develop') can be allowed for ('On Mondays he joins red group for level 2 work on money, on the other days he does maths with blue group who are working on level 3 number').

Some attainment targets require that the target is developed through children working with others. For example, in English (attainment target 1, level 1):

Pupils talk about matters of immediate interest. They listen to others and usually respond appropriately. They convey simple meanings to a range of listeners . . .

(DFE 1995 English: 26)

In a number of cases (for example, design and technology, and science) references to group working in original documentation have been taken out in the revised National Curriculum programmes of study. Similarly, the slimming down of the National Curriculum has led to a reduction in explicit references to group work as possible ways of developing a target. Teachers might of course choose to teach programmes of study using group-learning experiences even when these are not explicitly required or suggested. In mathematics, for example, children might work as a group in developing and explaining bar charts, although that target or corresponding programme of study does not refer to group work.

EVIDENCE ABOUT GROUPING OF CHILDREN SINCE THE INTRODUCTION OF THE NATIONAL CURRICULUM

Published evidence about the impact of the National Curriculum on classroom grouping is equivocal. Andrew Pollard and his co-workers found that key stage 1 teachers (interviewed in 1990 and again in 1992) believed they were doing more whole-class teaching in 1992 than they had been doing in 1990. This finding was based on teachers' reported perceptions, not necessarily what was taking place in their classrooms. In a parallel study, these researchers monitored 9 key stage 1 classes in 1990 and 1991. This observational study found a decrease in whole-class interaction and a slight increase in group work between the two sets of observations. (See Pollard *et al.* 1994 for a discussion about possible reasons for the apparent discrepancy.) There were very wide differences between practice in different schools. The researchers' concluded that, overall, there were fewer whole-class sessions in 1991, compared with 1990, but in 1991 a higher proportion of these sessions were used for teaching purposes.

Rosemary Webb (1993), monitored the implementation of the National Curriculum at key stage 2 in 50 schools during 1992–3. She found that although whole-class teaching was the predominant organisational strategy, teachers used a variety of methods and mixed whole-class approaches with various bases for grouping (for example, carousel, cooperative and menu systems). There were no teachers who supported streaming. This contrasts with the reported views of David Hart, general secretary of the National Association of Head Teachers, who was said to believe that streaming 'would prepare children for the shock of transition from the enjoyable hubbub of the child-centred primary classroom to the competitive, curriculum-based rigour of the secondary school' (*Times* editorial, 4 November 1991).

IMPLICATIONS FOR PRACTICE

Sarah Tann (1988) makes a useful distinction between the grouping of children that is an organisational matter, such as seating children around tables, and those work groups in which children work collaboratively. The two aspects of grouping are not synonymous. Children in primary classrooms are often seated in groups but work independently (Galton *et al*. 1980, Tizard *et al*. 1988). It is the second aspect, working as groups, which is considered here. These working groups can be subdivided broadly into cooperative and collaborative groups. In cooperative groups children work on separate and different tasks but these are finally pooled to produce a joint product. An illustration of this type of group is children producing a play in which individuals have taken on different tasks. In collaborative groups children work together on the same task to produce a shared result and the separate contributions cannot be readily disentangled. For example, children might work together, carrying out joint planning, exploration and trials, to design safe fireworks to be enjoyed by very young children. In practice a group project is likely to involve frequent switching between cooperative and collaborative working.

Working groups based on children with similar levels of attainment in particular aspects of the National Curriculum

Some areas of the curriculum are likely, for at least some of the time, to be developed by children working in groups with others at similar attainment levels. The individuals in these groups are likely to vary across different subjects and even within a subject. Although it might be easier in organisational terms to have children in the same broad ability-based groups for all curricular areas, most primary teachers do vary the children in different groups. This helps to avoid the labelling of children and encourages all children to see themselves, and to be seen, as able to do well at some things.

It might be argued that one disadvantage of the shared National Curriculum for all children is that it makes it more obvious that, especially in a mixed-ability class, some children (or perhaps only one child) may be carrying out the kind of work which classmates had completed a year or more previously. However, before the National Curriculum had begun, children as young as 5 or 6 rapidly realised the relative academic standing of classmates. This occurred even in mixed-ability classes in which teachers had tried not to draw attention to children's different levels of attainment. In one study (Crocker and Cheeseman 1988), 141 infant school children were asked to rate every child in their classes as better or worse than themselves. There was a strong agreement between self, classmates' and teacher's rankings and, from the age of 6 onwards, spontaneous rankings tended to be based on academic criteria. This supports what teachers often suspect: the academically less able children in the class tend to be quickly labelled as such by themselves, classmates and the teacher. This puts a responsibility on the teacher not to reinforce such rankings and to recognise the need to be consistently positive towards a child. Frequent, small, correct steps can be praised while large, incorrect steps can easily lead to a cycle of negative feedback, despair and further negative feedback.

It was common practice in the 1960s and 1970s to withdraw from the classroom children with particular difficulties. Withdrawal group work focused on intensive teaching, usually related to reading, and was often carried out by a peripatetic reading teacher who was not on the school staff. This practice came into disfavour because gains made in withdrawal groups were not sustained once children returned full time into ordinary classes. Other disadvantages of the withdrawal group system for children with learning difficulties are that those children miss out on normal classroom activities while they are withdrawn elsewhere, and they may experience conflicting teaching approaches and a lack of continuity in curricular content. The withdrawal group system also took attention away from the normal classroom in which the children still spent most of their time, so that ways of helping the child within the classroom (for example, by ensuring that classroom notices could be interpreted by all children) were not tackled. In addition, responsibility for children with learning difficulties came to be seen as outside the work of class teachers and, arising from this, was excluded from issues about whole school policy.

These difficulties have led to a move away from withdrawal group work and towards an emphasis on helping all class teachers to meet the needs of children with difficulties in learning. This emphasis has been sharpened in the 1994 Code of Practice which includes detailed guidelines about class teachers' responsibilities in identifying and assessing special educational needs of children in their classes. These are in line with what is being suggested in this book.

Special needs 'support' teachers now often work in the classroom alongside the class teacher. However, research by Caroline Gipps and her co-workers (1987) found that primary teachers

favoured withdrawal group work. It was the second most preferred strategy as a way to help children with special educational
needs; only smaller classes were seen as a more useful strategy.
The placing of these two strategies first and second is probably a
reflection of the huge demands on teachers' time in normal
classroom life. Anything which relieves these demands, such as
having fewer children around, is likely to be welcomed. It seems
that the in-class support movement is working against strong
enthusiasm for withdrawal group work but discussion among
school staff may clarify for whose benefit the withdrawal group
work is taking place.

For some children there may be a case for their working in a
small group with a special needs teacher, perhaps outside the
classroom, for part of the time. A study of children with communication problems in reception classes (Clark *et al.* 1984) lends
support for some intensive small group work on language outside
the classroom. The common framework provided by the National
Curriculum aids this type of activity by giving a structure of
continuity and progression. The central issues are not about where
the children work but about the degree of continuity across
different teachers and a belief that all teachers have responsibility
for children with special educational needs. It is vital that, if
children do participate in group work outside the classroom, one
person (for example, the class teacher) retains a clear role as
coordinator and manager of all the work in which each child is
engaged. This is considered further in Chapter 8.

Working groups based on children with a range of attainments

Some activities lend themselves to being developed in groups in
which children fulfil different roles, and the breadth of attainments and interests is an asset both in cognitive and social terms.
If children in a lower attainment group for one subject are in mixed
attainment groups for other curricular areas then the problems of
lowered self-esteem often found in streaming are less likely to
occur. Some primary schools are deliberately increasing mixed
aged, and by implication mixed ability, classes in order to spread
the load of assessments to be made at the reporting ages. For
example, where years 1 and 2 children or years 5 and 6 children
are grouped together, the teacher is involved in making end of key
stage assessments on only some of the children in the class. If all

year 2 or year 6 children are in single age group classes then their teachers have to make end of key stage assessments on the whole class during a relatively brief period (see Chapter 10).

Mixed attainment groups are important for children's personal and social development and should be used for at least some classroom activities. As children do work out the differences in the relative academic standing of classmates, it seems futile to try to pretend that these do not exist. A more positive response is to foster a classroom climate in which there is an acceptance that all children (and adults) have strengths and weaknesses; through this, individual differences are recognised not ignored.

A further advantage of mixed attainment work groups occurs if they are linked with a degree of autonomy and choice for children. If children work only with others of similar attainments then opportunities to see later stages of the learning are missed. A family session in a municipal swimming pool is a good illustration of a mixed attainment group. The pool will probably contain apprehensive non-swimmers, tentative doggy paddlers and efficient freestylers. Many adults state that they learned to swim not by being taught directly but by watching and then trying to imitate swimmers at their local pools. One might argue that they would have learned more efficiently with direct teaching in a group of similar non-swimmers. Both strategies have their place but self-initiated learning in a mixed ability group has the advantage of being paced by the learner and can build confidence not just in the task learned (for example, swimming) but in the process of being a learner. Swimmers who learned to swim by watching others are often very proud that they taught themselves in this way.

Work groups, which comprise children of varying attainments and incorporate individual choices, encourage children to try out ideas on one another and to extend their learning without necessarily having to go through the teacher to achieve this. This autonomy is important, given that teachers have been found to overestimate the learning needs of children with learning difficulties and to underestimate relatively able children (Bennett *et al.* 1984). Mismatching is likely to be diminished if children have opportunities to develop their own interests within structured guidelines, perhaps (depending partly on age range) contributing to a common goal. Chapter 6 contains examples of topic-based activities in which children of differing attainments could work together. Children with learning difficulties may lack confidence in their abilities and therefore their choices of activities in mixed attainment groups need to be carefully monitored so that confidence is developed.

Neville Bennett and Allyson Cass (1988) investigated the effects on group processes of different types of threesomes (including similar and mixed attainment groups; the latter being one high attainer with two lower attaining children, or, one low attainer with two higher attaining children). In similar attainment groups, the group of high attainers out-performed low or average attainment groups (in terms of quality, and quantity, of talk; recall, and reasoning, about decisions taken). The mixed attainment groups produced some thought-provoking findings. On every criterion studied the group comprising two low with one high attainer was superior to the two high/one low group. The researchers concluded that when two high attainers worked with one low attainer, the latter child tended to be left out. The findings did not support the idea that higher attaining children will lose out in mixed attainment groups. High attaining children, irrespective of group membership, performed well whatever the composition of the group.

Pairs of children working together

Various types of paired learning have been carried out with children with learning difficulties. Peer tutoring (Allen 1976, Topping 1988, Biott and Easen 1994) is one well-known approach which has, in various guises, been used by teachers of mixed ability classes. 'Peer' tutoring also occurs across classes, so that older children with learning difficulties tutor younger children with lower attainments than themselves. Peer tutoring, or similar types of activity, are a useful means through which children with learning difficulties practise skills that they have already acquired. Peer tutoring may also help the generalisation and application of these skills. These are aspects, as discussed earlier (Chapter 3), which are vital in the consolidation of learning and are very important for children with learning difficulties who need regularly to practise generalising and applying skills and knowledge. Some schools have developed 'shared reading' time in which, for a short period, all children in the school are paired and one child reads the book to his or her partner. They then discuss the book and perhaps change roles.

Peer tutoring involves an unequal relationship between the tutor and the tutored, as one child (the tutor) has skills which the tutored child clearly lacks. Some writers (for example, Glynn 1985) have criticised this approach because the child being tutored is always dependent on the child tutor. This criticism can be avoided if all children have the chance to take on the roles of both tutor and tutored. For example, 7-year-olds might be paired every Monday with 9-year-olds for tutors and on Thursdays, as tutors themselves, with 5-year-olds. A variety of research has shown that even children as young as 4 or 5 are adept at making appropriate adjustments in the way in which they talk to other children, differentiating between able and less able listeners and older or younger children (discussed in Wood 1988). These abilities have also been demonstrated by young mainstream children when communicating with classmates with severe learning difficulties (Lewis 1995c). The 6–7 and 10–11-year-old mainstream children whom I recorded were skilful in rephrasing instructions when working with partners with severe learning difficulties. They often shortened an instruction when it seemed not to have been understood. For example, 'Give me that long pencil from the box' was changed to 'Give me that one' (pointing). Vocabulary which was likely to have been difficult to comprehend was also changed. For example, one child said to her partner, 'Colour in the circle' and then changed this to 'Colour in the round'.

A different type of paired learning (sometimes called collaborative learning) occurs when two children of similar attainment levels work together on a problem. The roots for this work are in 'post-Piagetian' studies of young children's cognitive development and the view that cognitive development takes place when one child is challenged cognitively by another. This happens when one child is only slightly more advanced than the other. (The research has been reviewed by Wood 1988.) It is difficult to apply the research directly to typical classrooms but one important point is that children benefit from having opportunities to work in a *variety* of individual, paired, small group and whole-class contexts. A mix of these groupings, used flexibly, is likely to foster both cognitive and social development. Record sheets which show children's experiences of different types of group help to prevent a situation in which, by default rather than planning, children spend much time in individualised work. This applies especially to those who find school-based learning difficult. Unless there is deliberate planning for group work, these children may spend nearly all learning time in carefully planned and appropriate, but ultimately isolating, individualised programmes. This then compounds the difficulties that children with learning difficulties often have in developing social relationships with classmates. (The same difficulty arises in relation to able children given highly individualised work.) The playground may become the only opportunity for group activity.

A SPECIFIC ISSUE CONCERNING GROUPING: INTEGRATING CHILDREN FROM SPECIAL SCHOOLS OR UNITS INTO MAINSTREAM CLASSES

The points discussed earlier in this chapter apply to working groups which contain children who work part time in the class because they spend part of the time in special schools. However, there are some additional points, which concern integration generally, which can be made in the context of how children are grouped for teaching.

There are positive aspects of the National Curriculum in relation to integration (these are discussed more fully in Carpenter and Lewis 1989, and Lewis 1991). The implementation of the National Curriculum has not stopped special and mainstream schools from developing links. Evidence from a survey by the National Foundation for Educational Research indicates that the integration of children from special into mainstream schools has continued and, overall, links have increased since the introduction of the National Curriculum (Fletcher Campbell 1994).

Importantly, the National Curriculum provides a common language for detailed discussion of curricula across mainstream and special schools. The fact that it is common to both sectors not only helps mainstream school teachers to recognise that what happens in special schools is not totally different from what happens in mainstream schools but also helps special school teachers to see links between what they do and what is happening in mainstream schools. This, as noted in Chapter 5, is also important at the level of pupils' perceptions.

The National Curriculum also provides a series of common

curriculum ladders for all children, whether they are in main-stream or special education settings. The National Curriculum Council's Circular 5 (1989a) explicitly includes, within the common curricular framework, children with severe or profound and multiple learning difficulties (SLD or PMLD, respectively). This is a radical stance and shows how far thinking about those children's educational needs has come because, until 1970, those children were regarded as coming under the aegis of Health rather than Education authorities.

If there is integration between special and mainstream schools, and if foundation subjects are the foci of that integration, then it is likely to be helpful if there is a common curricular framework. The National Curriculum makes it easier to develop continuity and progression across special and mainstream school curricula for individual pupils. The importance of this is illustrated in Neville Bennett and Allyson Cass's (1989) case studies of children transferring from special to mainstream schools. Curriculum continuity was described as poor for three of the five children studied. Problems were particularly acute when the transition was made at mid-secondary, rather than the junior/secondary transfer stage.

The use of National Curriculum levels to guide curricular decisions across mainstream and special schools is described by Mick Archer (1989). He comments that a teacher from a special school is able to match the curricular needs of a pupil from the special school with what is offered by the mainstream school (and vice versa). Thus a child from the special school on, say, level 3 of the science curriculum can be placed in a mainstream school class in which level 3 science work is carried out. However, the possible dangers of imbuing National Curriculum levels with spurious accuracy should be borne in mind (see Chapter 5). One of the unresolved problems of the single eight (previously ten) level scale has been that (for example), in practice, level 4 at key stage 3 has often not reflected a similar level of attainment to level 4 at key stage 2.

Children of differing levels can work together effectively on a common task, drawing on different but complementary skills. This is another application of the paired or mixed attainment work groups that were discussed earlier in the chapter. In one inte-gration project (Lewis 1995c), involving 6- and 7-year-olds in a first school and peers with severe learning difficulties, staff decided to encourage the children to work cooperatively in pairs comprising a child from the mainstream school and a child from the SLD school. An example of a collaborative activity which was used in this project was wax-resist painting. In this activity the child from the mainstream school wrote his or her name or that of his or her partner in wax on a white sheet of paper. The child from the SLD school then painted over this. It was the responsibility of the mainstream school child to write both children's names on the picture when it was dry. This idea can be applied to tasks within the National Curriculum. For example, a game for a pair of children involving the making of 3D shapes from 2D card or plastic shapes could require one child to sort the shapes by colour or by shape (Mathematics attainment target 3, levels 1 and 2) and the other child to build the shapes into, for example, pyramids or cubes (Mathematics attainment target 3, level 4).

CONCLUSION

This chapter has reviewed various aspects of the National Curriculum in relation to the grouping of children at both a broad organisational level of allocating children to classes and, more narrowly, work groupings within classes. The tacit support given in the National Curriculum to collaborative group or paired work is a feature which should work to the benefit of all children. In addition, the 'hands-off' approach to deciding on teaching method emphasises the freedom and responsibilities of teachers in exercising their professional judgement in this area.

Chapter 8

Resources

The focus of this chapter is on ways through which we can make the most of resources, both human and material. I start from the premise that we are not likely to see major increases in funding for staff or materials and that therefore obtaining the maximum benefit from the resources that we do have will be crucial.

PEOPLE

The first part of the chapter will focus on several connected issues:

- making the best use of available adults in the classroom;
- the role of a coordinator for special educational needs;
- staffing for children integrated from special schools;
- classmates as a resource;
- care-givers;
- support services.

Making the best use of available adults in the classroom

The traditional picture of the class teacher working alone with his or her class for the whole school week is gradually being eroded. The 1987 primary staffing survey (DES 1987a) found that in England 18 per cent of full-time infant class teachers and 39 per cent of full-time junior class teachers did some teaching of children from other classes. Time spent teaching in other classes was usually brief (between one and three hours in the survey week).

Another change in primary classrooms over the last decade has been the increase in the range and number of adults in the classroom at any one time. This has led to an expanding of the class teacher's role to encompass not just teaching but also activities arising from collaboration with a diverse group of adult co-teachers and helpers. Collaborative working with other adults in the classroom is still not a major part of primary teaching. Jim Campbell and Sean Neill (1994) found that approximately one primary teacher in six reported teaching jointly for more than two hours a week. Approximately one teacher in five had more than five hours a week working with paid assistants. Adult co-teachers and helpers are likely to be involved with children with learning difficulties because class teachers often feel that it is these children who, in particular, need additional adult help. The Code of Practice (DFE 1994a) is likely to intensify this as it draws attention to the need for the school to monitor closely children identified as having special educational needs.

Adults who work in the classroom alongside the class teacher and who might spend at least part of their time with children with learning difficulties include:

- peripatetic support teachers for children with learning difficulties;
- peripatetic support teachers for children for whom English is a second language (some of these children may also have difficulties in learning);
- bilingual teachers based in the school;
- curriculum support teachers working to develop school policy in a particular curricular area;
- a school curriculum coordinator for a particular curricular area;
- members of a teacher support team, oriented to work with children with special educational needs, based within the school;
- other teachers in a shared open-plan base;
- educational psychologists;
- special needs specialists such as speech therapists;
- classroom assistants/ancillaries;
- nursery nurses (NNEBs);
- pupils from local schools;
- young people on work experience programmes;
- higher education students (some of whom may be on teacher-training courses, others may be studying for qualifications in parallel fields such as social work or psychology);
- care-givers (some of whom may be qualified teachers);

- school governors (some of whom may be qualified teachers);
- visiting teachers from other schools;
- miscellaneous visitors, some of whom may carry out some teaching (for example, older people considering training for teaching);
- people on licensed, or articled, teacher schemes.

A first step in coordinating the contributions of this diverse group of people is to establish the particular strengths of these individuals (for example, music, technology), so that these can be utilised to complement the work of the class teacher. Next, it is useful to identify which of these people will work regularly, and which irregularly, with the class. This will influence the types of activities and roles which the class teacher plans for and with these adults. It is crucial that the class teacher (or one specific class teacher, if teachers are working in a collaborative team) retains overall responsibility for coordinating the work of individual children with difficulties in learning. Such a task can be very time-consuming so, and ideally, primary teachers should have time away from teaching to carry out this role.

Although there are potential advantages in having a number of adults with a class, there are also possible difficulties. These include conflicts between the adults, confusion for children because conflicting information is given by different adults, children 'playing off' one adult against another, uncertainty about individual adults' roles, and a feeling by some adults that they are not wanted or needed. Time spent with children may be replaced by time spent organising adults and this may be unsatisfying for the teacher. Thus, initial enthusiasm for co-teaching may pall as the associated demands for sustained communication between the adults are not met.

Some of the ways in which teachers can support adults working in the classroom with children with special educational needs include:

- ensuring those adults are clear about their roles;
- providing regular opportunities for planning and discussion;
- providing positive feedback to those adults;
- making sure that those adults know the learning implications of children's special educational needs;
- making clear and realistic requests;
- providing training opportunities;

- integrating and valuing adult helpers as part of the team working with children with special educational needs.

(See Fox 1993 for a development of these ideas in relation to special support assistants.)

There are also issues concerning relationships between care-givers who work in the classroom and care-givers of children in the class. Kath Beck (1989) has discussed some of the dilemmas which can arise. She quotes a parent who expressed suspicion about confidentiality: 'Is a problem about my child discussed between a helper-parent and teacher?' (Beck 1989: 11). Another parent reported some grounds for this type of concern: 'There was an incident recently where one lady was discussing the skills, and the lack of them, of the children she had worked with. It was very unfair on the children, who were doing so well. Several mothers heard this and were quite annoyed, which is understandable' (Beck 1989: 12). All classroom helpers and teachers should be aware of this issue and be alerted to the need to avoid passing on judgements about children, staff or other care-givers.

Regular adult co-teachers

The increase in the number of adults working in classrooms, plus accumulating evidence of the amount of time that primary teachers spend within the classroom on administrative tasks, points to the need to rationalise tasks allocated to adults in the classroom. One way in which to coordinate the work of teams of adults is to assign specific roles to each co-teacher. (I am using the term 'co-teacher' for any adult, not necessarily formally qualified as a teacher, who works in the class as a teacher.)

Judith McBrien and Jane Weightman (1980) and Gary Thomas (1988, 1992) have described a useful way of planning for groups of adults to work together in a classroom. They have identified three specific roles which might be taken by the adults. These roles are: an 'individual helper', an 'activity manager', and a 'mover'. Gary Thomas (1988) focuses on an 'activity period' in which adults are allocated these specific roles. It would be feasible to apply these, for example, to an afternoon in which several adults regularly worked with one class. The individual helper(s) works with a succession of children, giving specific and detailed individual teaching. The activity manager(s) looks after the rest of the children in the class. Ideally, these children should be working on activities to which they have already been introduced. In terms of the model (Haring *et al.* 1978) discussed in Chapter 3, the children should be at fluency, generalisation or adaptation levels of learning in these activities. The mover(s) aims to maintain the flow of activity in the class by dealing with minor distractions, such as a note brought in from another teacher, a child who feels ill, or pencils needing to be sharpened.

This approach has wide application in that these three basic roles could be taken by a range of adults. Some of the 'mover' role might be taken by children. The system is adaptable and could suit different classes so that in a particular class the teacher could plan to have certain sessions in which there are, for example, two individual helpers, one activity manager and one mover. This type of systematic allocation of roles could go a long way towards resolving some of the potential difficulties of several adults working as co-teachers in a class. It would still be important for the class teacher to coordinate, explain and take responsibility for the system. Jean Gross (1993) makes the important point that children should be asked how they feel about the extra help given to them. Children's responses may contribute to the teacher's decision-making about the most effective deployment of classroom adults.

Glenys Fox (1993), drawing on developments in Hampshire, has produced some useful materials concerning special needs assistants working in partnership with teachers. The materials are applicable to other groups also. She lists some questions that support assistants might ask to clarify ground rules when working in classrooms. These questions include:

- How shall I be introduced to the class?
- How do I work with other pupils?
- Can I give pupils permission?
- Can I 'mark' books?
- Where shall I sit in the classroom?
- What shall I do if I see some misbehaviour?
- What is the best use of my time?

It would be valuable for anyone working alongside teachers to consider such questions and for teachers to be clear about what their responses to these questions would be.

Irregular adult co-teachers

The approach described above is appropriate if individual helpers come regularly. It is less feasible if help is erratic and individuals rarely work regularly in one class. Then, a more useful approach may be to focus on a development of the individual helper role. Some schools have developed individual 'task cards' or 'day books' for children, in which their work for the day, or perhaps work for a specific curricular area, is given. This enables any adult helping in the classroom to pick up the card or book and know immediately on which learning targets or activities a child is working. Figure 8.1 shows the type of task card which could be designed for a child in a primary school class. The card could be filled in by the class teacher each week and placed in a folder which is open to all adult helpers. There might be several children in the class for whom the teacher maintains this system.

RICHARD   Date: Week beginning 4 February

Handwriting is the main focus for additional help this week. Please check that 'o' and 'u' are being written in correct direction. Also pencil grip is poor; needs lots of practice in correct pencil hold and position when writing. Develop flowing writing movements with variety of pencils/pens.

Maths: developing work on number patterns. Understands the 2, 5 and 10 patterns. Needs help with '3', started this last week but still very unsure. Go on to 6 and 9 after this. Check that he understands by using blocks.

Language/literacy: making a book about insects. Has interviewed all the children in the class about their favourite/disliked insects, part way through block graphs to show the results. Headings for graphs needed. Also some discussion about how to interpret the block graphs. Wants to write a story about an ant in a jam factory, needs help with individual words for this. Encourage him to use a picture dictionary and the word lists around the class to help with these.

Finished last reading book. Encourage free choice from blue box in book box system (i.e. at a parallel level to the book just finished).

(Science: joining in group project on lcoal woodland. Next activity will be to make detailed observational drawings of a 1-metre square patch.)

Figure 8.1 Task card for Richard

The approach has worked well in a range of schools. In some, the cards or books were kept by the children, rather than centrally by the class teacher, and co-teachers talked to the child about selected areas for extra help. In either case, adult helpers have specific foci for their help and feel that they are fulfilling a useful role. They get to know well the individuals with whom they are working, and the children, for their part, enjoy the 'special' help. This is coordinated by the class teacher who amends the cards or books as necessary.

It may be useful to produce specific information booklets for adults working with individual children. For example, staff in Hampshire local education authority have produced a helpful series of special needs booklets for such people. These booklets include material relating to particular conditions, such as autism, and a guide for workers in the school transport escort service. This booklet has wider relevance and contains clear and useful advice including information about the use of physical restraint, and responding to a child who has an epileptic fit.

If the picture presented here is of the burden of working with, and organising, other adults in the classroom, then it is important to stress also the benefits of working alongside other adults. Jenny Nias's (1989) work on teachers starting teaching is very illuminating and illustrates how supportive such adult co-teachers can be. Nearly half of the inexperienced teachers in her research attributed their survival in their first posts to help from one or more specific colleagues. The adults who gave help were not necessarily teachers; classroom assistants, for example, were reported as being very valuable in helping the newly qualified teacher to 'learn the ropes'. Similarly, Colin Biott and Patrick Easen (1994) discuss collaborative working in schools and highlight the ways in which, through this, trainee and novice teachers are inducted into the rituals and expectations of the school.

Staff from local education authority support teams may be working in the class from time to time with children with special needs or, more indirectly, through giving advice about special needs provision. A 1990 survey by HMI of the work of advisory teachers for special educational needs drew attention to the diverse ways in which such teachers may work with class teachers (DES 1991b). HMI stressed the importance of an agreed policy between peripatetic staff and school staff concerning the aims and objectives of collaboration. Three-quarters of the lessons observed in which advisory teachers were teaching (this included in-class and withdrawal group work) were judged to be satisfactory or better. In fact nearly half of these lessons were judged to be outstanding. The quality of INSET provided by the special needs advisory teachers was generally rated highly by HMI. Eighty-two per cent of INSET sessions observed were judged to be satisfactory with nearly three-quarters of these rated as of very good quality. These findings are important given the demands facing schools through the implementation of the Code of Practice, and this survey evidence suggests that local authority support teams are, in general, a valuable source of information and guidance.

The role of a coordinator for special educational needs (SENCO)

The school coordinator for special needs should be a key person in helping all staff to make the most of opportunities for children's learning. The development, and numbers of, special needs co-ordinators in primary schools were discussed in Chapter 1. The demands, and possibilities, of this coordinator are extensive. The Code of Practice (DFE 1994a) advises that the coordinator will have to keep a register of pupils with special needs; liaise with colleagues, parents and external agencies; be responsible for the day-to-day operation of the school's special needs policy; co-ordinate provision for children with special needs; help to write individual education plans and contribute to the in-service training of staff. Key activities for the special needs coordinator are likely to include:

- Maintaining a register of children in the school thought to have special educational needs.
- Monitoring and reviewing curricula of individual children. In the context of the National Curriculum this may encompass helping staff to differentiate the National Curriculum in appropriate ways.
- Planning how end of key stage assessments might be carried out with children with particular difficulties so that the children work as well as possible and are not upset by tasks which are beyond them.
- Coordinating work within the school for the full range of

children with special educational needs, including any links with special and cluster schools.

- Leading revision of relevant school policy.
- Advising colleagues on particular special educational needs approaches and techniques.
- Providing SEN-related INSET to colleagues; for example, through the fostering of teacher support teams within schools (Daniels *et al.* 1993) or as part of cluster school provision (Lunt *et al.* 1994).
- Teaching children with special educational needs in collaboration with the class teacher. This may be one of the more daunting aspects of the role. Viv King (1989) has outlined various ways in which teachers might work collaboratively within the classroom. These include: one teacher leading and one supporting, the class working in mixed ability groups and both teachers circulating, either teacher targeting particular pupils, halving the class and working 'in tandem', one teaching and one observing/assessing, and a 'double act' in which the two teachers work jointly.
- Attending and reporting back on special educational needs courses and workshops.
- Knowing and understanding the relevant aspects of the 1988 and 1993 Education Acts, including the Code of Practice, in relation to children with special educational needs.
- Liaising with care-givers and outside agencies (notably Health and Social Services) working with children with special educational needs. In a minority of cases the special needs coordinator may, with the consent of the child's parents, need to liaise with the child's general practitioner.
- Giving information to governors and keeping them informed of the scale and scope of work in the school relating to children with special educational needs.
- Providing governors, especially a designated subgroup with a particular special needs remit, with detailed information about the range of support services needed by and/or available to the school. The extension of governors' powers to include budgeting makes this important, as provision for children with special educational needs is often a very expensive item for, perhaps, relatively few children.
- Liaising with voluntary groups, and the Named Person nominated by the local education authority, who may provide information to parents about special educational needs.

- Becoming involved in obtaining additional resources from voluntary agencies; for example, some schools have obtained grants from national 'Children in Need' appeals. Schools are also eligible to apply for funds raised through the national lottery. This does raise political issues about whether or not it is right to draw on money from charities to help fund a state education system.
- Collating evidence relating to cases taken to the regional special needs tribunal.

The above list is a very extensive set of responsibilities. A recent survey of special needs provision in mainstream primary schools found that many of these activities were already carried out by many special needs coordinators, often in conjunction with another role (Lewis 1995a). The implementation of the Code of Practice (DFE 1994a) is likely to lead to further demands on the special needs coordinator. It will not be possible to meet these demands if that role is tied to full-time class teaching or to an additional major responsibility such as headship, especially in a medium or large school. HMI's survey of children with statements of special educational needs in mainstream schools noted that, where the special educational needs postholders were allocated time to pursue their duties (such as advising and supporting colleagues and organising identification, assessment and review procedures):

> it was possible for pupils and staff to be effectively supported, good practice disseminated and school procedures established and followed.
>
> (DES 1990d: para. 32)

The Code of Practice (DFE 1994a) has advised that school governors should recognise the demands of the special needs coordinator's post in allocating staffing. It is hoped that governing bodies will be sufficiently sensitive to special needs issues to maintain or create a post in which these can be developed alongside, say, a half-teaching timetable.

Staffing for children integrated from special schools

A specific aspect of staffing for children with difficulties in school-based learning concerns children who have statements of special educational needs under the 1981 or 1993 Education Acts. By definition, these children have learning difficulties which require special provision to be made for them. Children with statements in mainstream schools might be registered full-time in the mainstream school or might be on the register of a special school or unit and attend a mainstream school for part of the school week. I shall describe the latter as 'child-based link schemes' to distinguish them from 'adult-based link schemes' in which it is staff rather than pupils who move between special and mainstream schools.

Discussion of placements in special or mainstream schools overlooks a shift towards increasing child-based link schemes. These are hidden when data report only schools in which children are nominally registered. The NFER research into links between mainstream and special schools (Fletcher-Campbell 1994, Jowett et al. 1988) found that link schemes were widespread. Brian Goacher and his co-workers (1988) also found that most special school heads reported increased links with mainstream schools. There has been much debate about the rationale and effectiveness of child-based link schemes. The Select Committee on the working of the 1981 Act (House of Commons 1987) took the view that link schemes were an important aspect of integration. Whether special school, mainstream school or some child-based link scheme between the two is the best option for a child and his or her family will depend on a range of factors, including staff attitudes and resources. Some writers (for example, Moore and Morrison 1988) argue that advocates of child-based link schemes are taking a weak view of integration and that the children from the special school are always visitors, rather than genuine classmates, in the mainstream school. As such, child-based link schemes constitutute only partial integration and sustain, rather than diminish, segregation.

Some local education authorities have made extra staffing available to foster educational integration. This has taken various forms, including an integration support teacher who accompanies groups or individual children from a special to a mainstream school, who gives advice to the mainstream school and/or teaches collaboratively with mainstream school teachers. (See Carpenter et al. 1988 for a fuller discussion of the role of an integration support teacher.) Special support assistants may be provided to help children with particular needs; for example, arising from physical disabilities.

Where specific additional help is provided for children with learning difficulties in mainstream schools, there may be issues about whether the individual adult(s) works only with the statemented child or with a range of children. This raises complex issues and has, in some instances, led to complaints by the child's care-givers that the terms of the statement are not being met because specific additional help (for example, three hours per week for individualised programmes) is not being given. The closer and better the relationship between the school and the care-givers, the less likely it is that such an issue will arise. For example, if a child with severe learning difficulties has a special support assistant for, say, ten hours per week (two hours each morning), then, unless it is clearly specified in the statement, the class teacher (in discussion with others) will have to decide what is the best use of that help. It may be totally within the classroom and with that child alone, it may be within the classroom with a small group including that child, or it may be with the child in a withdrawal group for specialised teaching. (See Chapter 7 for discussion about withdrawal group work.) It seems reasonable for the special helper to work with other children while the class teacher works with the statemented child. This would also help to avoid a sense of over-possessiveness between the statemented child and the special support assistant, leading to covert segregation within the classroom.

The issues are not just about the amount of individualised teaching but also about the quality of the teaching received by children with learning difficulties. The need for mainstream school teachers to receive advice about teaching children with severe learning difficulties is evident from HMI's survey of 43 primary phase schools attended by a range of children with statements of special educational needs (DES 1990d). This survey found that there was wide variation in the effectiveness of mainstream school placements for statemented children but that, in general, children with sensory impairments or speech and language difficulties received work which was better matched to their needs than did children with severe learning difficulties. The survey found that additional teaching support was sometimes provided by classroom ancillaries. These people had had no in-service training in the role and 'There was evidence that a lack of knowledge and skill could result in inappropriate intervention in activities thus inhibiting pupils' progress' (DES 1990d: para. 37). It is clearly crucial that all staff, including classroom assistants, special support assistants and nursery nurses working in the classroom, are included in in-service training.

Classmates as a resource

Classmates are a potential resource for all children. If the classroom climate is one in which children are encouraged to work together, then one child helping another child with, for example, spellings is not conspicuous. Thus a child with learning difficulties being taught by another child is just a natural part of the classroom ethos. Similarly, if it is recognised that all children can give and receive help in different ways and for different tasks then children with difficulties in learning are likely to experience both sides of this. As discussed in Chapter 7 in relation to pupil grouping, it is important that they do experience both the giving and receiving of help.

There are several ways in which, within the classroom, this type of strategy can be encouraged. For example, some teachers have a 'rule' that children always ask one another for help before they ask an adult. The sharing and reporting back of work is a common practice in many primary schools and encourages children to be positive about what other children have done. The mutual support provided is especially important for children who, through repeated difficulties in school tasks, may have become apprehensive about revealing their work to other children. Many schools have fostered shared learning in which children work together on a task. This can be developed so that children produce materials, such as stories, for other classes or other schools. 'Round robin' stories, in which successive classes or schools add to a continuing story, have become popular. Some schools have developed desk-top publishing ventures, enabling the final class or school to reproduce the story/newspaper for all of the children, classes or schools involved. Gerda Hanko (1985), Sarah Tann (1988), John Thacker (1990), Elizabeth Dunne and Neville Bennett (1990), Maurice Galton and John Williamson (1992) and Colin Biott and Patrick Easen (1994) have all discussed group learning in classrooms. They provide useful analyses and ideas for practice.

Care-givers

The importance of liaison with care-givers was discussed in Chapter 4 in relation to identifying where children are in their learning. The ways in which care-givers might work within the classroom has been discussed earlier in this chapter, but not all care-givers are able or willing to work in the school. Much of children's learning is stimulated by what happens at home and, generally, schools now work hard at developing and sustaining links between home and school. This may be done for educational reasons, such as enhancing children's reading through various 'home reading' schemes. It may also be done for political reasons. A variety of legislation (notably the 1986 and 1988 Education Acts) has given care-givers and school governors greater power and influence over what happens in schools. This orientation is continued in the Code of Practice (DFE 1994a). The Code suggests that schools' arrangements for the parents of children with special needs should include information in a range of community languages, information on tape for parents who have numeracy or literacy problems and a parents' room (or other arrangements) in the school to help parents feel comfortable. Communication needs to be two-way so it is not just information from school to home which has to be accessible to parents. In addition, information from home to school has to be made accessible to relevant staff at the school.

There have been many imaginative schemes to develop home–school links (see Wolfendale 1983, Topping and Wolfendale 1985, Widlake 1986, Bastiani 1987). In the present context, attention is specifically on ways in which care-givers can help to develop the learning of children who find school tasks difficult. An important aspect is sustaining the child's motivation for learning. This is a two-way process; the school may explicitly develop interests begun at home and the home may extend school-based learning. The range of activities which children carry out with care-givers, siblings, other family members or friends can be a rich basis for applying and generalising skills and knowledge. If teachers and care-givers do not meet, then informal notebooks or audiotapes sent between home and school can help to sustain two-way communication. This is especially important if the child is unable or unwilling to talk to care-givers or teachers about what he or she has done at school or home.

Gerda Hanko (1985) has written of the specific issues surrounding collaboration with care-givers of children who have difficulties in school-based learning. School staff may feel wary about collaboration because they anticipate that care-givers will attribute the child's difficulties to poor teaching. Discussing this openly means that teachers may have to face searching questions about what and how they have been teaching. Requirements to report to care-givers about children's progress on National Curriculum attainment targets may increase this. Research into the progress of children through infant schools (Tizard *et al.* 1988) found that the teachers rarely explained teaching methods to care-givers. Care-givers may have different ideas from the school about the best way of helping a child with difficulties. One parent commented, 'I want to work with the school but I don't like it that he's treated differently from the others, I don't like it that he has his own special desk' (Sedgwick 1989: 127). Meanwhile, the care-givers may fear that they will be seen as the problem and blamed for the child's difficulties. There are grounds for these fears. Paul Croll and Diana Moses (1985) asked 428 junior school teachers about hypothesised causes of difficulties in learning. Home factors were thought to be the cause of slow learning or poor reading for one-third of these children. Home factors were given as the cause of emotional or behavioural difficulties for approximately two-thirds of children with these problems. Home factors may be a contributing cause of difficulties but are outside the teacher's control. Genuinely collaborative home–school relations will help to diminish negative stereotyping of care-givers of children with difficulties in learning and to foster joint planning of constructive strategies.

Support services

There is a wide range of support services available to teachers. Many of these include a focus on promoting educational opportunities for children with learning difficulties. In most local education authorities these support services have included: school psychological service (sometimes still known as a child guidance clinic), school health service, speech therapists, education welfare service, peripatetic support teachers ('remedial service'), special school outreach workers, inspectors/advisers with responsibility for children with special educational needs, professional development centres and curriculum support teams. Some of these services have different names in various local education authorities. For example, Caroline Gipps and her co-workers (1987) found 35 alternative names in use for 'peripatetic remedial services'.

A range of additional support services (such as medical, social and/or psychiatric) is directed to individual children. There is also a wide range of national groups, mainly voluntary, which provide information, advice and materials concerned with the education of children with specific difficulties. (See Male and Thompson 1985, Darnbrough and Kinrade 1985, Leclerc 1985, TIPS [Dawson 1985], DFE 1994e for details about many of these groups.) The importance of voluntary groups may well increase with the implementation of the Code of Practice (DFE 1994a). At stage 4 in the stages identified in the Code:

> LEAs should (also) give parents information about independent advice, such as local or national voluntary organisations and any local support group or parent partnership scheme, which may be able to help them consider what they feel about their child's needs and the type of provision they would prefer.
>
> (DFE 1994a: 40)

In response to this, some local education authorities are developing posts for liaison between school and voluntary groups. Also, many parent groups concerning children with special needs are likely to be active in setting up local groups.

HMI (DES 1989h) surveyed support services for children with special educational needs and concluded that service provision did make a difference to the schools and pupils who received support. HMI found that most schools would not have been able to bring together the range of expertise and resources that was evident in the majority of the support services which HMI visited. A survey by Malcolm Garner and others (Garner *et al.* 1991) found that most local education authorities had adopted the model of one or more centrally organised and funded services for certain groups of children with special needs. Budgetary changes were seen as likely to jeopardise the retention of a range of central special needs support services. It is evident that schools, particularly small schools, value these services (Weston *et al.* 1992).

MATERIALS

The second part of this chapter considers the material resources available to help a teacher to provide children with suitable opportunities for learning. Two aspects are considered: first, briefly, the variety of materials available and, second, a way of organising and coordinating some of these resources.

Range of available resources

Local support services, such as those listed above, may loan materials as well as, or instead of, people to foster the educational opportunities of children with learning difficulties. In particular, special school outreach services and peripatetic support services for children with learning difficulties have, since the 1988 Education Act, been producing curricular analyses of ways in which programmes of study might be made accessible to children with learning difficulties (see Chapters 5 and 6). Professional bodies for teachers concerned about children with learning difficulties provide advice and, in many cases, publish relevant materials (see Leclerc 1985). In addition, the national bodies referred to under support services sometimes have specific resources available.

Coordinating materials

Eldridge Cleaver said, 'There is no more neutrality in the world, you either have to be part of the solution or you're going to be part of the problem – there ain't no middle ground.' One way in which teachers in primary schools can be 'part of the solution' in helping children who find school-based learning difficult is through the effective organisation of relevant resources. This section describes an approach to coordinating resources, for children with learning difficulties in primary schools, in ways which are consistent with the demands of the National Curriculum.

The class teacher may be on the receiving end of a great variety of materials in connection with enhancing educational opportunities for children with learning difficulties. The approach described here is one way in which different materials could be combined into a single, coordinated and coherent system. It could be incorporated into different types of classroom organisation, including subject-based or cross-curricular, whether organised around individuals, 'mixed ability', or 'similar ability' groupings. The ways in which resources are organised do not dictate methods of learning but they should enhance the opportunities for learning, whatever the teaching style. The approach has been used widely in a variety of primary and special education settings. It aims to make good use of the time and resources available without isolating children with learning difficulties from their classmates. The approach also reflects the need for both structure in children's learning and breadth of teaching methods.

Research into the effectiveness of different teaching styles and surveys by HMI about successful classroom practice repeatedly emphasise the importance of a variety of teaching methods in promoting children's learning. This has been discussed in Chapter 6 and is mentioned here in order to put into context the approach described for coordinating classroom materials. It is a system which lends itself to relatively narrow and specific skills. Much classroom learning is not of this type, but some is, and for those areas it is a useful approach. Phonological awareness, handwriting, spelling and some number skills are particularly appropriate foci of this very structured approach. However, all of these need to be supplemented with broader-based approaches.

Opportunities for learning are enhanced if the relevant resources are clearly organised and accessible to children. At a basic level this means having routine classroom materials, such as scissors and paper, clearly labelled with pictures as well as written notices to show what goes where in the classroom. At another level, learning materials also need to be clearly organised. This is not a problem if all, for example, mathematics work is done from one central scheme but, as the diversity of materials and teaching methods increases, classroom organisation becomes a critical factor in promoting or limiting learning. I have discussed the possible range of adults in the classroom who may need to draw on a common pool of resources for work with children with learning difficulties. A good test of the clarity and coherence of the way in which learning materials are organised is to ask: if a supply teacher were to take over the class, would he or she be able to find, quickly, appropriate learning materials for children with (for example) spelling difficulties? This is a reasonable question to ask. An HMI survey of children with special educational needs in mainstream schools (DES 1989a) found that, in 18 per cent of the primary schools surveyed, pupils with special educational needs were being taught by supply or temporary teachers on the day that HMI visited. The primary staffing surveys (DES 1987a, WO 1988), carried out in March 1987, found substantial numbers of staff absent. In England and Wales approximately half of the schools surveyed (58 per cent and 46 per cent respectively) had staff away during the survey week. Supply teachers were used extensively to cover for these absent staff (64 per cent of all absences in England and 41 per cent in Wales). This snapshot does not show the picture over time but in-service training linked to the National Curriculum and Code of Practice, as well as usual absences through sickness, is likely to have increased the use of supply and temporary staff.

All children need regular teachers with whom they can build up warm and positive relationships but this need is particularly important for children with learning difficulties who, as discussed in Chapter 3, often lack confidence in learning and find it very difficult to generalise skills and knowledge from one context to another. For children who find school-based learning difficult, a succession of teachers presenting slightly different ways of, for example, setting out and carrying out vertical addition sums can limit progress because the children fail to make links across the different strategies.

A second test of the organisation of materials for children with learning difficulties is to consider to what extent the children are able to find appropriate materials for themselves. If children can find their own learning resources then they can take some control of their own learning, instead of being dependent on the class teacher. Children with difficulties in learning have often had relatively little autonomy because their apparent need for help has been seen as evidence that more, not less, teacher direction is needed. Thus, while other children choose project work topics or reading materials from a broad range, children thought to have learning difficulties have a much narrower choice or even no choice at all. There is an intrinsic dilemma. To give freedom of choice of learning materials may be to permit, perhaps encourage, inappropriate choices which will in the end be counter-productive. If 'free choice' leads to a child opting for relatively easy materials then the activity will not move on the child in his or her learning. If relatively difficult materials are chosen then confidence may be lost and learning does not progress. The skill is to provide choice within a structured framework so that genuine choice is possible but leads to an activity which matches the child's learning needs.

The first stage in organising resources is to find (or write) the outline of the school's curriculum (schemes of work) and any work outside the National Curriculum. Parts of these schemes may need to be subdivided into smaller steps (see Chapter 5). This division into smaller steps is the second stage in coordinating resources. The nature of the steps will depend on the curricular area. Some skills lend themselves to a hierarchical sequence (for example, addition of numbers) but other areas of skill or knowledge (for example, developing creative writing) can only be divided tentatively into wider areas of progression towards the learning target. Ideally the staff in a school should work together to decide on which areas to focus for subdividing. The choice will depend on the priorities of the school and its community. Many staff will probably want to begin by subdividing early aspects of the core subjects. The initial division will probably be quite crude, perhaps using ideas such as those in *A Curriculum for All* (National Curriculum Council 1989d) or in Chapter 5 here as starting points. Magazines such as *Special Children* and *Support for Learning* have also contained articles outlining possible subdivisions. Locally, support services may give advice and perhaps possible ways of subdividing parts of the programmes of study which are relevant to the school's schemes. Some special schools for children with moderate or severe learning difficulties have made this type of advice available to local mainstream schools.

In many schools, sound–letter links ('phonics') has been an area in which children with difficulties in reading have been given specific and detailed help. This aspect of the curriculum lends itself readily to the approach described here, which would need to be used alongside broader approaches to developing reading. *Phonics and Phonic Resources* (Hinson and Smith 1993), published by the National Association for Special Educational Needs (NASEN), provides a possible sub-division (58 steps) concerning phonological awareness. These 58 steps are not necessarily sequential, although they form a broad progression from auditory discrimination to multi-syllabic words. These steps fit well with the broader levels identified in English for key stages 1 and 2 (DFE 1995).

Having identified aspects of the school's schemes which have been subdivided into smaller steps suitable for children with learning difficulties, the next stage is to link materials with each step in the curriculum. This stage is likely to involve considerable discussions among staff about the suitability of materials. The NASEN book of *Phonics and Phonic Resources* cross-references a wide range of resources for each of the steps identified. It is useful to extract names of materials found within the school and to compile a class or school index of resources. Materials lost or later regarded as inappropriate can be deleted and later additions can be included as they are found or made. The pages can be kept in a binder with a removable plastic spine so that individual sheets can be rewritten if necessary. The phonics teaching should be carried out alongside other work to develop reading and writing. This example relates to phonological awareness but the approach is applicable across a wide range of curricular areas (see Turnbull 1981 for application to mathematics).

Each step in the school's scheme needs to have some type of simple coding which can be cross-referenced with relevant materials. This could be done in the same way in which books have been grouped in a 'book box' system, whereby books with similar reading ages are grouped togther and a child chooses a book from a particular level rather than working through one specific scheme.

The clear organisation of resources, which are allied to steps in the curriculum, enables the learner to find materials independently of the teacher. This encourages children's autonomy and allows the teacher to teach rather than to manage resources. The children who will themselves be using the system will often have good ideas about how it should be organised. It is important that a wide variety of types of material is included at each step, as, otherwise, a child might use specific, narrow approaches to the exclusion of other materials. It is not the aim of this coordination of resources to have children working tediously through masses of arid materials. For example, early addition might be developed through: microcomputer programs (individual or group), maths games (individual or group), taped exercises or games (individual or group), games/activities using other audiovisual material (for example, synchrofax, *Language Master*), workcards, worksheets, and book extracts from various schemes (if necessary cut up so that only work of a similar level and focus is on one card/sheet). All of these could be coded to link with the appropriate step in the school's scheme and place in the National Curriculum. A page on early addition in the resource book could list all of these materials and/or the materials could be grouped together physically.

The materials might be stored in one central place in the school so as to be shared by all classes or, depending on the numbers of children to be using the system and/or on the geography of the school, the materials might be shared by only a few classes. The storage area could be relatively large, for example, a converted cloakroom space, or something more modest, such as a filing cabinet or trolley, depending on what is feasible and realistic for the school. Resource banks which are not in a classroom might need to be monitored for part of the time by an adult. However, in schools which have developed this system, an adult has been needed only to monitor the use of the resource bank in the early stages, as the children have quickly become used to the system and been able to use it responsibly and independently. The retrieval of materials from the resource bank is a useful skill for children to acquire and this type of activity is explicitly included in the programme of study for Reading, key stage 2:

> Pupils should be taught how to find information in books and computer-based sources by using organisational devices to help them decide which parts of the material to read closely . . . Pupils should be taught to use library classification systems, catalogues and indexes.

(DFE 1995 English: 14)

When resources have been grouped and linked with specific parts of the curriculum then gaps-may become apparent. Supplementary materials can be produced to fill these gaps. For example, it might become apparent that whereas there is much material on 'magic e', there is very little material to help children's recognition of 'silent letters'. Similarly, if the approach includes materials relating to science, some topics (for example, 'weather') may be included in a comprehensive and detailed way while there is no breakdown of, for example, how to help children to understand the idea of forces in science. Supplementary materials might be very specific and might need to be made by people working in the school, perhaps using some of the adult helpers identified earlier in this chapter. Other materials might be obtained from the local support services.

This approach to organising and coordinating resources has several advantages. Single copies of incomplete sets of materials, which are of little value on their own, can be incorporated into a larger system. Inspection copies, review copies, and home-made materials can all go into the 'bank'. Teachers often make small sets of workcards or have ideas for games for children having specific difficulties – for example, to help a left-handed child with writing, or to help a child to learn a set of sight vocabulary words. Concrete materials might be made to help a child to grasp concepts about, for example, place value or word 'families'. These sets of materials are often not used again and the work is lost. If they slot into a coherent system then they can remain useful and accessible. Children who like learning through a particular medium are able to use their preferred approach as much as possible while still focusing on a learning task which is appropriate for them. Most importantly, children have access to a wide range of materials in learning an area, so that they do not have to keep using the same materials with which they have already failed to learn. Whole staff discussions about coordinating resources are important because they help the staff to gain ownership of the system of resources. An imported package might be easier and quicker but it is less likely to be used or to be used effectively.

One danger in the cross-referencing of materials as described here is the possible confusion, for children with learning difficulties, arising from the use of different conventions in materials from different sources. Different print styles are a notorious stumbling block for children just beginning to interpret print. Similarly, terms might not be interpreted as synonymous (for example, 'add', 'add on', 'go on', 'increase', 'go up', 'add up', 'move on', etc.). Teachers, parents and others involved in compiling resource banks need to look out for, and exclude, materials which use styles, terms, or notations which conflict with those of the school (for example, a French '7' in mathematics materials). Some schools have sheets of 'agreed' number/letter symbols, and terms (for example, 'multiply' rather than 'times'), so that all staff explicitly use the same style. This helps to avoid children misreading or miswriting, for example, 3 and 5; 4 and 9; or L/I and 1.

CONCLUSION

The emphasis on progression and continuity in the National Curriculum should minimise unnecessary repetition of the early stages of learning for children with difficulties. Teachers are generally quite good at identifying broadly which children find school-based learning difficult. This needs to be extended so that individual children are matched with appropriate learning experiences for particular curriculum steps. This is important, as inappropriate materials may lead the child (or any learner) to feel frustrated and unmotivated. When the available materials have been coordinated in this way, the teacher might decide to add some way of identifying at which point the child is in relation to the particular steps. This relates to many of the points discussed in Chapter 4 but in the present context some specific 'game' cards might be made to assess individual steps. This approach is one way in which teachers in primary schools could organise learning materials to meet the needs of children with difficulties in learning. It is probable that only a small number of children will require this system at any one time so it is reasonable to pool resources across several classes. It is not being suggested that most children will need this approach. Indeed, it is likely that the small curricular steps linked to specific materials and activities would be counter-productive and, for many, would slow down learning. Neither is it being suggested that children with learning difficulties should spend a disproportionate amount of time working through such a system. It will be important to add activities which help children to generalise and apply the skills practised. The effectiveness of this approach depends in part on how well it helps the teacher to monitor, and respond to, children's learning. This leads to issues about record keeping which are the focus of the following chapter.

Chapter 9

Record-keeping and reporting

Why bother with keeping records about what children are learn-ing or have learned? Teachers sometimes say that they can remember what they need to know about children's learning without spending time writing down detailed records. If that approach was ever sufficient, the 1988 and 1993 Education Acts, specifically the National Curriculum and the Code of Practice (DFE 1994a) have ensured that it is not enough now. The ex-student teacher who told me that he was not going to keep records of children's learning because he planned to become an inspector would find that the need for records, at any level, is increasing rather than diminishing. Carolyn Blyth and Fiona Wallace (1988) found that reception class teachers considered it necessary for nurseries to maintain and to pass on records concerning children with special educational needs. The reception class teachers preferred not to be 'prejudiced' by receiving records on other children. Some teachers might disagree with the latter point but the findings do illustrate an implicit recognition of the particular importance of monitoring and recording the learning and develop-ment of children with special educational needs.

Classroom records may be prospective (for example, teaching plans for the long, medium or short term) or retrospective (for example, children's learning, including developmental changes and curriculum-based assessment). Sometimes a short-term teach-ing plan can double as a record of a child's learning in specific activities. The focus of this chapter is on records of children's learning rather than on the writing of teaching plans. The latter has been discussed in Chapters 3, 4 and 5.

This chapter is in four parts: the first outlines requirements and practice concerning records of children's learning in the National

Curriculum, the second discusses the purposes and types of records of individuals' learning which are maintained by the teacher (often in cooperation with care-givers), the third part of the chapter reviews ways in which children might maintain their own records and the fourth section summarises requirements concerning the school's register of children with special educational needs. Broader issues about record-keeping which are applicable to all children (for example, the general form of reporting to care-givers) will not be explored in detail. The materials on teacher assessment from the School Examinations and Assessment Council (1990a) examine questions and possible practice concerning whole-class and school record-keeping.

THE NATIONAL CURRICULUM AND RECORDS OF LEARNING

Nick Yapp, in *Bluff your Way in Teaching*, suggests that the purpose of record-keeping is: 'To make sure that teachers don't nip off at half past three every day' (Yapp 1987: 42). Record-keeping, he says, is a chance to fantasise and to write down what was supposed to happen, what the teacher wishes had happened, and what the teacher knows will never happen. Circular 8/90 (DES 1990f) sets out to curb such flippancy in relation to records of children's learning.

Research by Ted Wragg and his co-workers (1989) found that 55 per cent of teachers, in a sample of 901 primary teachers surveyed, anticipated that record-keeping, in relation to the National Curriculum, would be difficult (48 per cent) or very difficult (7 per cent). Work by Sarah Tann (1990) suggests that this concern about record-keeping continued once the National Curriculum had begun. She found, in a review of the first term of the National Curriculum in infant and first schools, that adequate monitoring and recording of children's learning were the teachers' chief concerns. There is, on the basis of evidence from HMI surveys, grounds for these concerns. HMI's first survey of the implementation of the National Curriculum (surveyed Summer 1989) noted that:

> The most common forms of record keeping . . . did little to inform either future planning or provision in the core subjects.
> The great majority of schools fell short of what is required to

fulfil the requirements of the National Curriculum, particularly in science. There is a need for greater clarity about the purposes served by records, for whom the recorded information is provided and the uses to be made of it.

(DES 1989c: paras 38, 42)

HMI's second report on the implementation of the National Curriculum (surveyed Autumn 1989) indicated that the National Curriculum was having a major impact on record-keeping: 'About four fifths of the schools were in the process of introducing new record-keeping policies or establishing revised arrangements' (DES 1990g: para. 36). This endorses a comment by the National Curriculum Council (1989f) that teachers would need to 're-structure' record systems to bring them into line with the National Curriculum. However, HMI had doubts about the quality of this restructuring:

Nearly a half of the new arrangements were, however, regarded as ineffective or inadequate. Most criticisms were directed at checklists, some of them very detailed, which provided only superficial information about the specific skills and levels of understanding and knowledge acquired by children.

(DES 1990g: para. 37)

Despite these criticisms, HMI concluded that, overall, methods of record-keeping had improved since the previous term (i.e. the Summer 1989 survey). Positive developments included: greater standardisation of records; a wider range of areas recorded (both within and outside the core subjects); and the use of National Curriculum attainment targets, rather than place reached in published schemes, as the foci of records.

However teachers in some schools tried to keep records in too much detail and they focused more on what teachers had taught than on what children had learned. There is a consensus that the least useful form of learning record is the ubiquitous tick list on which the teacher notes what has been 'done' rather than what individual children have learned. OFSTED (1993b), reporting on children's attainments in a sample of urban schools, noted:

[Primary] teachers gave a high priority to hearing children read but their records noted usually only what they had read and not their level of skill . . . Recording systems mostly took the form of subject tick sheets which indicated that attainment targets had been covered in class but not how well individuals had performed.

(OFSTED 1993b: paras 19, 23)

Ron Dearing's final report (SCAA 1994b) discouraged the over-zealous recording of attainments. Teachers were reminded that records should be useful, manageable and easy to interpret. This was probably the position held by most teachers until, through the complexity of the National Curriculum statements of attainment, teachers had felt obliged (or were misinformed about the need) to exceed this. Ron Dearing's report noted that there was no need to keep records that were superseded by later progress, no need to write long narrative descriptions of previously known information, no need to record the same attainment more than once, and no need to record curriculum coverage (only what children have learned). It is worth bearing these points in mind when planning how to implement the Code of Practice (DFE 1994a). Otherwise this too may lead to over-ambitious attempts at detailed recording.

Records and accountability

The statutory position is that each governing body of a maintained school must keep a curricular record for each child registered at the school. Schools are also required by law to report annually, as a minimum, to parents about their children's attainments in all National Curriculum subjects and 'other activities'. This applies as soon as children commence National Curriculum programmes of study (i.e. from age 5 for most children). Reports at ages 5, 6, 8, 9 and 10 (i.e. non-reporting ages at key stages 1 and 2) can be in terms of subjects and/or attainment targets. These reports have to be updated each year. Ron Dearing's final report (SCAA 1994b) emphasised that how teachers record children's progress is a matter for schools to decide and that there is no point in abandoning workable systems. The law does not lay down how children's progress in attainment targets should be monitored and recorded during the course of a key stage.

Requirements concerning reporting at the ends of key stages 1 and 2 are complicated by the varying status of aspects of the curriculum. At the ends of key stages 1 or 2 (i.e. ages 7 and 11 for most children), the reports to parents must show:

- the results of nationally prescribed tests and/or tasks in the core subjects;
- the results of teacher assessments in the core subjects;
- a brief commentary showing what the above two sets of results show about the child's progress;
- comparative results for peers at the school;
- comparative results for the school, compared with national, data (it is difficult to see how schools can report comparative data in ways which do not undermine the confidence of children with learning difficulties);
- brief details about non-core subjects (there is no requirement to report National Curriculum levels for attainment targets in the non-core subjects so broader records could be kept here);
- other activities organised by the school.

Schools are required to meet reasonable requests from auditors or moderators for (a) samples of children's work arising from end of key stage assessments and (b) material supporting teacher assessments. There is no requirement to provide this evidence in any particular way nor to provide evidence to substantiate teachers' assessments of every child (DFE 1993, 1994f). Schools have been encouraged to keep school portfolios of work which has been assessed and agreed by all staff. This work, especially if it includes some from children with special educational needs, could provide a very useful reference point for all staff. In addition it has been suggested (SCAA 1993) that schools keep portfolios of a few pieces of work for individual children. The work chosen might be particularly good or especially significant for the child. Such portfolios, especially if they included the child's comments about the work, would make a useful addition to records for children with special educational needs. They could form part of stage 1 assessments of the Code of Practice (DFE 1994a).

Parents have a right to request, and to be given, information about their children's levels on individual attainment targets at the end of the key stages. Obviously this reporting will be eased if the teacher's formal records dovetail with the annual report forms. Some schools are using microcomputer programs to store and transfer these types of records. The notes kept by a teacher purely for his or her use are not a formal part of the child's curriculum record and so do not have to be disclosed.

Children with learning difficulties may, in order to demonstrate progress, require more detailed records than are needed for other children. Formal annual reports to parents or care-givers must include indications of any aspects of the National Curriculum that have been disapplied. If large parts of the National Curriculum have been disapplied then it is up to the school to decide what information to pass on to the care-givers. Circular 8/90 states that:

It must be a matter of good practice for schools to amplify with narrative commentary . . . the reports on all pupils with learning difficulties which lead either to exemptions (whether on individual or multiple attainment targets) or to slow progress from one level to the next.

(DES 1990f: para. 21)

It would be logical and sensible to link these records closely with annual reviews for children who have statements of special educational needs. The statement should, by law, be reviewed annually and the teachers' records will be important in showing whether learning targets have been met and how, if at all, the statement should be amended. However, research into the working of the 1981 Education Act (RDAMP 1989) found that statements tended to be written vaguely and so masked discrepancies between a child's needs and the available provision. Similarly, HMI's review of children with statements in ordinary schools found that statements were of 'mediocre quality . . . lacked detail, gave little guidance on the pupil's curricular needs and were inadequate for the planning of an educational programme' (DES 1990d: para. 45). Thus, a benefit of the National Curriculum may be in sharpening considerably the wording and foci of statements although, for many children, targets will be wider than the National Curriculum (for example, including social and self-help skills). The implementation of the Code of Practice (DFE 1994a) should also diminish vagueness in formal statements of special educational needs.

Practicalities

There is a need to think imaginatively about how time can be created for essential non-teaching, but teaching-related, activities. Some local education authorities have allocated assessment/recording support teachers to give class teachers time for observation, assessment and record-keeping for, say, half a day each week. Greater use of collaborative teaching, in which two (or more) teachers work jointly with their classes, might encourage more flexibility of teaching group size and so give time for one teacher to carry out assessments and record-keeping. The use of various adults in the classroom (discussed in Chapter 8) might also mean that some kinds of record-keeping could be done by an adult other than the class teacher. There is also room for using audio and video records as well as, or instead of, the more usual written accounts. A good video of, say, a class drama or science project can convey more vividly than can a written account the breadth and depth of learning taking place. This could form a focus for sessions giving feedback for care-givers or governors and could also be loaned to families for them to watch at home.

Some schools have 'star child' meetings in which all staff meet to discuss individual children's learning. Usually staff will meet for a short while (perhaps just 15 minutes) on one or two mornings per week, before school starts, specifically for 'star child' sessions. Teachers take it in turn to review the learning of several children in their classes so that all staff can share relevant information, offer suggestions and keep up to date with individual children's progress. If all staff are involved, including ancillary and support staff, then a broad picture of the child can be shared. Inevitably the children who feature in star child sessions tend to be children who stand out in some way, perhaps because they are causing concern or are the focus of a statement of special educational needs (or, perhaps, of temporary exceptions for disapplication of the National Curriculum). The star child discussions run a risk of reinforcing prejudices unless they are chaired skilfully; the discussion leader needs to ensure that assertions and reports are supported with evidence and that the discussion focuses on the positive and the relevant. Given these provisos, star child sessions are potentially an excellent way of drawing together information from a range of people who have worked with the same child at different times and in various situations. Usually such sessions are not formally minuted and so are not a part of formal, written records.

Greater use could also be made of diary records between home and school to which care-givers, teachers and children all contribute. These can form a natural record of children's learning and development and are especially useful for children who say relatively little to parents/teachers about what they have done at home/school. Sheila Wolfendale (1989, see also RDAMP 1989) has worked extensively on ways to amalgamate home and school-based information about children's learning. The *All About Me* profile is one approach which, like the diaries mentioned above, can be used for children starting formal schooling but has applications across the primary age range. Some schools for children with severe learning difficulties also use diary records to convey home–school information. Without these records there may be little information between home and school about the children's daily activities. This lack of communication arises from the children's poor memory or linguistic skills as well as the possible distance betweeen home and special school which means that the children are taken to the school by special bus or taxi, unaccompanied by parents/care-givers. If successive diaries are saved by the school, with other records, a broad account of the child's attainments and experiences may be stored.

RECORDS OF LEARNING/TEACHING MAINTAINED BY THE TEACHER

One of the main purposes behind record-keeping in schools is to maintain continuity and progression in children's learning. The centrality of these themes in the National Curriculum means that record-keeping has become a central issue in discussions about implementing the National Curriculum. Records of learning for children with learning difficulties may aim to fulfil some ad-ditional and very specific purposes. These include: monitoring learning in relation to particular learning targets, monitoring stages of learning, noting various factors which impede or promote learning (such as membership of specific work groups and the effectiveness of different teaching methods) and checking that the child experiences a broad curriculum on a daily and weekly basis.

The types of record which might meet each of these purposes will be discussed and possible outlines given for appropriate records. These outlines are given tentatively as possible starting points, not blueprints. Individual teachers will know what would fit their own ways of working. The need for teachers to devise record systems which suit, perhaps uniquely, their own schools, has been emphasised by Tom Christie (a member of the Manchester-based STAIR consortium which developed one approach to end of key stage assessments). He stated: 'I firmly believe that ultimately we need 25,000 recording systems. I believe it because I think that we need 25,000 different school environments' (Christie 1990).

Monitoring learning in relation to specific learning targets

Records of learning in specific curriculum-based activities are an important adjunct to broader and class records which include children with difficulties in learning. These can be developed with the school coordinator for special needs, as part of the school's implementation of the Code of Practice (DFE 1994a). A division of target activities into smaller steps (see Chapter 5) links naturally with a record sheet showing these steps and the child's progress through them. Such records need to show:

- possible sequence of steps for a particular learning target (bearing in mind that these are guidelines and that the child may jump around the steps, especially in activities, such as creative writing, which cannot be classified into a single hierarchical sequence);
- when the child started activities towards the target;
- teaching/learning approaches used;
- other information about the context and circumstances in which the learning took place;
- National Curriculum attainment targets to which the steps link;
- date on which the child was first able to complete the target;
- series of dates on which this achievement was checked;
- any links with the child's statement.

Some advantages of these records are that they:

- focus on what the child can do;
- have clear implications for teaching;
- build up into a detailed record of part(s) of that child's learning, showing continuity and progression;
- can be maintained by the teacher and child together;
- give the child frequent feedback about his or her progress;
- are individualised, so that one child is not being compared directly with other children;
- can be easily understood by care-givers and other adults (important if several adults work with the child; see Chapter 8);
- can show patterns over time (for example, that a child needs regular fortnightly revision of sight vocabulary words);

- can be used as evidence if they relate to a child's statement;
- can amplify other records used in conjunction with stages 1 to 3 of the Code of Practice (DFE 1994a).

Figure 9.1 is a sample record sheet which contains all of the features summarised, although this is at the expense of having much room to write. If classroom records are to be useful, they need, like Ordnance Survey maps or horse racing form books, to combine succinctness with good quality, relevant information and to be uncluttered by the irrelevant.

This degree of detail will be needed for relatively few children and for only some activities in most mainstream primary classes. It would be unrealistic and inappropriate to try to maintain records containing this much detail for all children in the class. However, if some records do contain this level of detail, they can

---

NAME: Sammy   CLASS: Year 3

POS: English, KS 1   ACTIVITY: Story → ATs 1/1, 1/2, 2/1

Programme of study   *Assessment*

Activities	Evidence of learning		Dates
Listen to story tapes and discuss with adult	Recounted one incident	○ ⊘ ●	10 Sept 14 Sept 1 Oct
Listen to story tapes and discuss alternative endings	Drew imagined next event	○ ⊘ ●	24 Sept 19 Nov
Invent stories using picture sequences	Told story from 3-picture sequence onto tape	○ ⊘ ●	24 Sept 3 Dec
Invent story from initial stimulus		○ ⊘ ●	

Observation notes and action:
Sammy enjoys puppets. Develop ways of using these to stimulate story telling. Sammy's parents keen to help Sammy at home with developing stories. Lend Sammy's parents story tapes from toy library to use at home. Discuss learning aims for Sammy with them, e.g. encourage Sammy's evaluation of stories.

Figure 9.1 Sample record sheet for an individual child having difficulties in a specific curricular area
(Key: ○ = begun; ⊘ = achieved; ● = checked)

double as both teaching plans and learning records. This approach was used in one school in which I worked. The children kept these records in their work folders (for core subjects only) and would work with the teacher to fill them in when an activity had been finished. These children, who were some way behind their classmates, seemed to obtain a sense of achievement as the columns were filled in. The small steps listed meant that most children moved quickly through them. More global targets would have taken these children many months or terms to move from one target to the next.

The least useful type of record is probably the extensive series of extracts from programmes of study to be listed for all children in the class and against which every child will eventually be ticked off. There must surely be a strong temptation to ignore for several months such an arid record and then to go through the whole class at some crucial date, such as before a parents' meeting, and quickly enter, perhaps undated, ticks and crosses for every child. The only use for this type of summary sheet is as an administrative record rather than as a guide for teaching; it cannot include the necessary detail about how, as well as what, children are learning. Detailed records such as those described earlier could provide information for a summary sheet.

Monitoring stages of learning

For some children, difficulties may arise because the children learn things initially but then fail to retain the skills or processes and/or cannot use them in new contexts. For these children it is useful to have record sheets which, again tied to specific activities, record various stages of learning (see Chapter 3). Figure 9.2 gives an example of a record sheet to record stages of learning.

Noting various factors which foster or impede learning

There is a strong temptation, when discussing records, to make the areas which warrant recording more and more numerous. All records are inadequate in that there is always more that could be said or written about individuals' learning. However, including comment about school-based factors which foster or impede learning is useful (see Chapter 4 for a discussion of some relevant factors) but is only worth while if the information is used. Some

NAME: Tracy A. POS: Maths, KS 2		CLASS: Year 3 ACTIVITY: Addition to 10→AT 1/1, 2/1, 2/2	
Programme of study		*Assessment*	
Learning stages	*Activities*	*Evidence of learning*	*Dates*
Acquisition	Add to 10, with teacher, using Unifix	Buitl tower of bricks, counted correct total (up to 12)	○ 15 Jan ⊘ 11 Feb ● 1 Mar ● 8 Apr
Fluency	Snap and other quick number games	Orally, added domino cards correctly (10 in one minute)	○ 7 Feb ⊘ 10 Mar ● 8 Apr
Generalisation	Shopping games in class 'market'	Added money correctly, using coins, totalling up to 10p	○ 4 Feb ⊘ 9 Mar ● 8 Apr
Adaptation/ application	Applying add facts in map drawing	Drew map of classroom, talked about equal sides 'made up' differently	○ 22 Apr ⊘ 25 Apr ●

Figure 9.2 Sample record sheet to show stages of learning for an individual child in relation to a specific curricular area (*Key:* ○ = begun; ⊘ = achieved; ● = checked)

writers refer to children with difficulties in learning as 'the hard to reach' or 'hard to teach' which, rightly, puts the onus on the teacher rather than the child.

Most teachers can think of children who, while making relatively slow progress in some curricular areas, do very well in others or in particular contexts. The process of writing down details about the contexts in which the child is successful helps to focus attention on these and therefore on how they might be maximised. A brief way of doing this would be to have a summary sheet of notes with the child's profile which contains helpful and limiting aspects of the classroom situation for that particular child, including specific and detailed evidence for the comment. Discussion with the child and his or her care-givers about more and less successful teaching methods helps to fill in the picture and to show whether suspected preferences or dislikes are confirmed by the child.

Diary-type records built up over time may also show significant patterns of behaviour which are lost in the more fine-grained records of curriculum-based assessment. If a child has a folder containing examples of his or her work from pre-infant school days onwards, then diary-type records can be added to the folder. This folder becomes a continuing record of a child's achievements and should include the child's evaluative comments about his or her work. Children with learning difficulties may have attended pre-infant school assessment units and, if so, information and possibly children's work from there can be included in this folder.

Checking that the child has a broad curriculum on a daily, weekly or termly basis

There is a variety of record sheets available for the National Curriculum. These range from photocopied sheets developed by staff in a particular school to glossy, commercially produced planning and summary grids. On the one hand, home-made record sheets are more likely to fit the purpose and to be used, but there is a risk of teachers spending time re-inventing the wheel; on the other hand, commercial schemes may appear to be definitive and foolproof, to save much agonising and tedious listing of attainment targets and so forth but they may be extremely boring and in the end may not be used very effectively.

The experiences from the trialling of end of key stage assessments and their accompanying record sheets show that teachers disliked the pro-formas provided and revised these. This might have been a reflection of the record sheets but it also illustrates the strong tradition of primary teachers constructing their own materials. Even local authority-derived National Curriculum record sheets, devised by teachers in the authority, are reportedly changed by other teachers using them in school. This seems to me to be a constructive strategy which helps teachers to have ownership of the materials and therefore to make better use of them. However, such individualism is at odds with pressures to use the National Curriculum to create greater uniformity across schools.

Most of the commercial and home-made record-keeping schemes which I have seen have focused on individual subjects, perhaps bringing together the three core areas in a summary sheet. Children with difficulties in learning have tended to do many activities in 'basic skills' at the expense of the broader curriculum (see Chapters 2 and 3) and record systems which emphasise the National Curriculum core may reinforce this pattern.

The appropriate record sheet for recording an overview of, say, weekly learning will reflect the orientation taken by the school towards planning the whole curriculum. For some schools a weekly check sheet might contain HMI's areas of learning and experience (DES 1985) while for other schools a simple listing of National Curriculum subjects, religious education and cross-curricular themes can be a useful antidote to curricular narrowing. This type of check could be used for all children but would be particularly important for children who, for example, repeatedly carried out additional English activities and for whom the teacher suspected that other areas were being neglected. The overview could be completed by the teacher (perhaps using two different symbols for work planned and for work actually carried out). This would show where a child avoided or favoured activities (for example, tending to carry out design and technology work in preference to written language, where both were possible activities, such as in the development of a cross-curricular topic). The teacher could choose to focus on two or three children each week when completing this type of record. Over a term all children would then have been recorded for one week and the children on whom there was a need to focus more strongly (perhaps because they were often absent) would have been monitored for two weeks. The record sheet could be completed through teachers' recalling activities done by children and/or by using children to make the record. The following section explores ways in which children can maintain records of learning goals and attainments.

RECORDS MAINTAINED BY THE CHILD

There are many ways in which children can maintain records of their learning goals and attainments. To do this ought to help both the child and the teacher. This section reviews four broad types of child-maintained records: records of the learning process (including goal-setting and attainments) in one activity, evaluative records of learning, daily or weekly records of activities carried out, and summative records of learning targets.

Child-maintained records are important because of the links with developing children's autonomy in learning and promoting self-confidence. Both of these are things which children who have had difficulties in mastering school tasks may lack and which therefore further impede learning. A vicious circle is created in which the child 'fails', loses confidence, becomes more dependent on the teacher, loses autonomy and so is back to greater dependence on the teacher. Turning this into a virtuous circle, in which success in learning leads to increased confidence and motivation and so to further learning, is one of the skills of teaching.

Child-maintained records in specific tasks

Some activities lend themselves to a record built up by the child which shows the process that he or she is going through in reaching a particular goal. For example, a story can be recorded in a zig-zag book containing successive versions (see Figure 9.3). This helps children to see how their work is developing. A similar approach can be used for successive plans in making a technological model. Children who perceive themselves as being of low ability seem to be particularly helped by seeing that an early, rough piece of work is part of the process towards a more polished, final version. Similarly, they see that all children go from rougher, early versions to more polished, later versions. Successive writers' drafts illustrate the same point (although the use of word processors may mean that this evidence is no longer being produced). One well-known children's writer sent extracts from successive drafts of one of his stories to a class which I taught. The children (all of whom had learning and/or behavioural difficulties) were astonished that a published author did not write the final story at his first attempt. They were surprised that, just like their first drafts, the author's early attempts at a story were messy and incomplete. This experience seemed to help them to accept that they also would make better stories by trying to improve first drafts.

Child-maintained evaluative records of learning

Children's evaluation of their own work can be linked to records. Peter Gurney (1990) has reviewed a range of research which investigated links between children's self-esteem and school achievements. He observes:

(a)

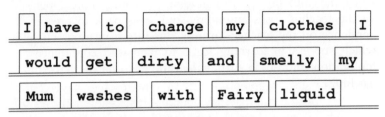

I	have	to	change	my	clothes	I
would	get	dirty	and	smelly	my
Mum	washes	with	Fairy	liquid

(b)

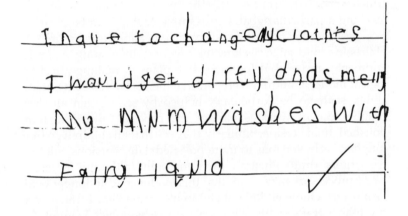

(c)

```
I have    to    change    my    clothes.

I would   get   dirty    and   smelly.

My Mum    washes    with    Fairy    liquid.
```

Figure 9.3 A record of developing a piece of writing (by Simon, age 8)
(a) Planning the writing using a *Breakthrough* folder (at a later stage,
making a handwritten plan)
(b) Writing the first draft
(c) Typing the draft into a word processor (at a later stage, making
improvements to successive versions)

Arrange for a failing child to achieve success in a task and what is he likely to say? 'It was a fluke,' or 'I was lucky.' The evidence of success is likely to be rejected because it is discrepant with his self-concept.

(Gurney 1990: 9)

Peter Gurney argues that it is important for teachers to help such children to shift to accepting that they themselves have control over the type of result that they obtain. A discussion with an adult about what is good about the work and how it could be improved helps to keep children's evaluations both recognised and realistic.

A primary school headteacher, Julie Barsby (1991), devised a series of ways in which children could evaluate their work. She was particularly interested in developing children's evaluation of their creative writing. To encourage this, she invented various gauges which were placed around the classroom. These home-made gauges included a device like a large toothpaste tube from which a roll of coloured cloth could be unrolled, an elephant with a retractable trunk, and a sequence of smiley faces. Each child, having completed some writing, would then go, with a friend, to one of these gauges, and discuss how the piece of writing was to be rated. Various criteria were discussed with the children before-hand and included: how interesting was the story, was it easy to follow, and could it have been made more exciting? The children discussed how far to move the indicator in order to give a rating on specific criteria for the piece of work. When Julie Barsby assessed systematically whether or not these gauges helped chil-dren to become more self-evaluative she found that their use was associated with more frequent and more appropriate evaluations.

Some schools encourage children to make evaluative comments about all their work (see Lawson 1992 and McNamara and Moreton 1993 for examples relating to children with special educational needs). When written work is completed, it is accom-panied by comments from both an adult and the child. Even if not all work is annotated in this way, it would be reasonable to do this for work which goes into a current folder of the child's work. If the school keeps folders of samples of children's work then individual children can choose, after discussion, which pieces of work should go into their folders. Similarly, classroom or corridor displays can include spaces for viewers' comments and these may be about the presentation as well as content.

Child-maintained daily records of learning and activities

Children can be encouraged to maintain their own daily records of activities planned and carried out. Although this applies to all children, it is particularly important for children with difficulties or disillusionment about school tasks because child-maintained records emphasise the child's active part in monitoring learning activities. One strategy involves children posting tickets when they have started or finished particular activities. For example, the teacher might set out various activities which are accompanied by pieces of card (colour coded for the activity: for example, blue for maths, yellow for reading, red for science). When the children have finished the activity, they write their names on the cards and post the tickets into a box or tray. The teacher then has a record, provided by the children, of who has been engaged in which activities over the session or the day. Another strategy entails children writing, on an overall plan, the activities in which they have been engaged. Some teachers begin the day by going through, with a whole class or group, the activities which individuals will be doing. These are written onto a sheet of paper, whiteboard or overhead projector transparency to form a timetable for the day (or week). As children complete their sections, they tick off their names.

Child-maintained longer term summative records

Children can keep continuing summative records of their learning. Some curricular areas lend themselves to a record sheet which shows successive steps towards various goals. An obvious example is a record sheet showing aspects of learning spelling or decoding parts of words. Figure 9.4 shows an example of a 'phonics' record sheet in which the teacher started by assessing the sounds which the child could decode. (The sequence of 'sounds' can be found in *Phonics and Phonic Resources* [Hinson and Smith 1993]; see Chapter 8.) Squares representing these known sounds were then coloured in by the child. As the child learned further sounds, these were also coloured in (and dated). Different colours were used for different terms in the school year so that the chart also showed some idea of the rate at which new sounds were being learned. The record was readily understood by the children and, as it was linked explicitly with the classroom resources,

PHONETIC RECORD SHEET:

1	2	3	4	5	6	7	8	9	10	11	12	13	14	15	16	17	18	19	20
vis. disc.	aud. disc.	cons	a	e	i	o	u	short vowel revision	b/d	ee	oo	$\overline{oo}$	ll ss ff	nt st ck	sh	ch	th	wh	ph

21	22	23	24	25	26	27	28	29	30	31	32	33	34	35	36	37	38	39	40
shr sch thr tch	pl fl cl	pr cr fr	sw sn sm	dw tw qu	scr spr squ spl	a-e	i-e	o-e	u-e	magic e revision	ai	ar	au	aw	ay	$\overline{ea}$	ea	er	ew

41	42	43	44	45	46	47	48	49	50	51	52	53	54	55	56	57	58
ie ei	ir	oa	oe ie ue	oi	or	ou	ow	$\overline{ow}$	oy	ur	y	pref.	suff.	kn mb ght wr	soft c+ g	-r	ms

Name:

Date started:

Figure 9.4 Example of a phonics record sheet on which children record their successive attainments

Source: Hinson and Smith (1993)

children could also tell from the chart which set of work they should go on to next.

It has become popular to encourage children to monitor their own learning but at times this seems to be done in a way which lacks much purpose or coherence. In one school, I saw children colouring in windows on a stylised drawing of a house (drawn and photocopied by the teacher onto individual sheets) to show how many stories they had written that week. As this had no qualitative aspect and was subsequently thrown away it seemed to have no value to either the children or the teacher.

REGISTER OF CHILDREN WITH SPECIAL EDUCATIONAL NEEDS

The Code of Practice (DFE 1994a) introduced the requirement that the school's special needs coordinator should have responsibility for keeping a register, and making it available, of pupils with special educational needs. Any child identified at stage 1 under the Code of Practice – that is, has given any reason to alert parents or professionals to potential special educational needs – should be included on the school's special needs register. Schools are likely to vary widely in how readily they place a child on this formal register of special educational needs. Once a child's name is placed on the register the coordinator should check with the class teacher, two or three times a year, to monitor the child's progress. Once it is clear that there is no longer any cause for concern the child's name can be taken off the special needs register. This will be after at least two review periods (i.e. about two terms). This might happen without any special intervention or after this has taken place.

CONCLUSION

Lesley Webb, writing in 1967, rated record-keeping to be as important as the teacher's personal attitudes in identifying children in need of extra help. While that function remains important, effective record-keeping is also vital in a climate of renewed accountability.

Chapter 10

Summative assessments at the ends of key stages 1 and 2

> It is not possible to describe a standard of attainment that should be reached by all or most children [by the end of primary school].
>
> (CACE 1967: para. 551)

This statement from the Plowden Report of 1967 stands in stark contrast to the orientation of the National Curriculum. The National Curriculum embodies continuous teacher assessments of children's learning, regarded generally as difficult but desirable and uncontroversial, and summative assessments at the ends of key stages. The purpose of the summative assessments, plus the conceptual and operational difficulties in combining formative with summative assessments, has been widely debated (for example, Nuttall 1988, 1989; Flude and Hammer 1990; Gipps and Stobart 1993; Gipps and Murphy 1994).

The assessments at the ends of key stages in the National Curriculum have been seen as serving, and shaped towards, summative/reporting, not formative/teaching, purposes. It is unusual to find, as in OFSTED (1993b), that teachers are reprimanded for not using summative assessments formatively. The emphasis on the function of end of key stage assessments as oriented to national monitoring, not the planning of individual's learning, is reflected in the recent requirement that end of key stage reports to parents must include comparative data about the child's attainments relative to his or her school and the national picture (see Chapter 9). Caroline Gipps and Gordon Stobart describe the position unequivocably:

> The aggregated summative information is there for accountability and political purposes; it is there to evaluate and monitor

schools rather than to help directly in the education of individual children.

(Gipps and Stobart 1993: 98)

This chapter looks first at the nature of summative assessment in the National Curriculum, then at some general issues arising. The following section reviews evidence, arising from the implementation of the National Curriculum to date, about summative assessments of children with special educational needs. The final part of the chapter examines implications from research evidence about ways to improve the validity and reliability of standard tasks when used with children with learning difficulties.

THE NATURE OF SUMMATIVE ASSESSMENT IN THE NATIONAL CURRICULUM AT KEY STAGES 1 AND 2

The nature of assessment in the National Curriculum is complex and confusing. Assessment is wider than, but encompasses, tests. Recurrent changes in terminology, requirements and practice have intensified the confusion and confounded perceptions of 'tests' and 'assessment'.

Summative assessment at the ends of key stages 1 and 2 comprises:

- nationally prescribed tests and tasks applied to some or all of the core subjects and some or all of the attainment targets within those subjects (pattern varying in different years and for different key stages). These tests and tasks have been referred to in early National Curriculum documentation, and by some commentators, as standard assessment tasks (SATs). More recently they have been called Standard Tasks (STs) or 'standard tests and tasks'. There is a distinction between 'test' and 'task'. At key stage 2 most pupils will take pencil and paper tests in the core subjects. 'Less able' pupils, defined as those working at levels 1 and 2, will take more practical, classroom-based, tasks. At key stage 1 there will be tasks for:
  - all children in writing,
  - children at levels 1 and 2 in reading, and
  - children at level 1 in spelling and mathematics.
  Children at higher levels in reading, spelling and mathematics at key stage 1 will take tests in those curricular areas (see DFE 1994f);

- teacher assessments, which may be moderated, applied to attainment targets in all three core subjects. These are reported separately from the results of standard tests and tasks;
- teacher assessments for history, geography, Welsh (where applicable) and design and technology. These assessments may encompass non-mandatory, but standard, tests and tasks as well as teacher-designed assessments; and
- teacher assessments, leading to reported end of key stage descriptions, for music, art and physical education. These assessments will be based on teacher-designed assessments.

Not formally included are religious education, cross-curricular areas excluded from subject-linked assessment, and broader aspects of education such as social and moral development. (See Gipps and Stobart 1993, OFSTED 1993c and Shorrocks *et al.* 1993 for overviews and analyses of summative assessment of children's learning of the National Curriculum.)

Independent schools do not have to participate in these assessment procedures although they have been encouraged to do so by the DFE and SCAA. If they do choose to be involved and their results forwarded for national data collection then they must take part in auditing procedures.

Foci of summative assessments

It is the standard, externally derived, element of the summative assessment which has been the most contentious. The foci of the standard tests and tasks have progressively narrowed since the recommendations of the Task Group on Assessment and Testing (TGAT) (DES/WO 1988). This report suggested that, at the end of key stage 2, three or four assessments might be made. These might focus on mathematical/scientific understanding, literacy and humanities, and aesthetics. These have been narrowed to some aspects of English and mathematics (for key stages 1 and 2) and some aspects of science (key stage 2). These assessments are all subject-specific and not, as advocated for key stage 1 in the TGAT report, cross-curricular.

Comparative status of curricular areas, as reflected in the assessment pattern

It has been argued by some commentators that the narrower foci of standard tests and tasks reflect the relative status of aspects of the curriculum. It has been suggested that areas seen by the government as being 'important' are being assessed through standard tests and tasks while 'less important' areas are left to statutory (but more subjective) teacher assessments or, even, non-statutory teacher assessment. For example, the exclusion of speaking and listening from standard tests and tasks may be seen as diminishing the importance of oral work and encouraging teachers to give less time to developing these skills. A more pragmatic response is that the piloting of end of standard assessment tests and tasks showed that, given existing staffing levels, it would be impossible to make standard tests and tasks as broad as originally envisaged (DES/WO 1988). On various grounds (for example, time, and distortion of the curriculum), any narrowing of standard tests and tasks could be interpreted as educationally beneficial. It means that those standard tests and tasks may be less intrusive. They may take up less time at the ends of the key stages and so free teachers to get on with teaching and evaluating the broader curriculum.

Another, perhaps cynical, response to the narrowing foci of standard tasks is to say that this reflects diminishing government confidence in the National Curriculum. If the assessment process is thorough, wide ranging, reliable and valid *and* it turns out that, over time, the National Curriculum does not seem to be raising standards, then the government has to defend this.

Balance between standard tests/tasks and teacher assessments at the ends of key stages

The successive narrowing of standard tests and tasks can be interpreted in various ways. At one level, it is an endorsement of the importance of teacher assessment. The balance between standard tests/tasks and teacher assessments has changed with a move away from nationally prescribed tests. This is likely to be welcomed by teachers of children with special needs as those teachers have urged that greater value should be placed on teacher assessments of those children (see, for example, NCC 1993a). Teacher assessments and standard tests/tasks now have equal weighting in summative assessments:

> The professional judgements that teachers make of their pupils' classroom work are of equal value to the results of national tests

and will be treated as such: test results and teachers' own assessments will be reported and published alongside one another.

(Shephard 1994)

Individuals to carry out the standard tasks

Circular 8/90 (DES 1990f) stated that at key stage 1 most teacher assessments and standard tasks would be carried out by the class teacher. In practice, a special needs support teacher might work through standard tasks with individuals or small groups of children, taking care that, for example, the language of the instructions has been understood. The support teacher might arrange for computer keyboards (including Concept keyboards), rather than pencil and paper, to be used as a means of recording.

SEAC (1990b) has advised that, if children usually have support staff help, that support should be there also when those children are involved in standard tasks. This could mean that, for example, a speech therapist rather than the class teacher might carry out the assessment task. This is an important aspect of helping children to show what they are able to do. However, if the school has single age group classes for children at the reporting ages, this may have the effect of concentrating support staff in a few classes while end of key stage assessments are being carried out.

GENERAL ISSUES ABOUT SUMMATIVE ASSESSMENT IN THE NATIONAL CURRICULUM WHICH HAVE IMPLICATIONS FOR CHILDREN WITH SPECIAL NEEDS

National Curriculum levels as end-points or stages

There has been inconsistency about whether the levels on attainment targets represent end-points or broad stages. This can be described as conceptualising the levels as either mile markers (see Figure 10.1(a)) or pathways between the mile markers (see Figure 10.1(b)). For example, if a child is described as being 'at level 2', does this mean that he or she has mastered material at that level or that he or she is working towards level 2? This issue was referred to in Chapter 5 in connection with planning learning. It

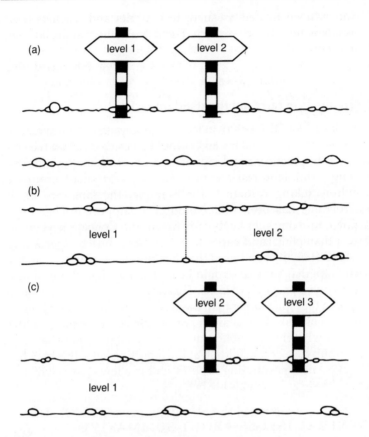

Figure 10.1 Levels on attainment targets
(a) NC levels as 'mile-workers'
(b) NC levels as pathways
(c) level 1 as a pathway and other levels as mile markers

is perhaps more critical in the current context, as it dictates the level at which the child is reported to be.

SEAC's early advice on National Curriculum assessment arrangements described the levels on attainment targets in terms analogous to 'mile markers':

> There are no intermediate points on the scale. A pupil is assessed as achieving a particular level – 2, say – when the relevant criteria are satisfied. Up to that time, the pupil is reported as having achieved level 1 and to be working towards level 2.
>
> (SEAC 1989: para. 6)

Thus, according to this advice, the criteria for the levels on attainment targets are minima, so that a child who is between levels would be described as being at the lower level. This stance is evident in circular 21/94 in which it is stated that at key stage 1 if a child is working towards level 1 in an attainment target, 'the child's level should be counted as zero' (p. 6–7). (This statement is omitted from the parallel section of the circular dealing with key stage 2 and so the position at that stage is unclear.) To count pre-level 1 as '0' seems to contradict other advice that a child who has not attained level 1 should be described as 'working towards level 1'. The 'working towards level 1' position rightly recognised that a child who has not attained level 1 may still possess considerable skills, knowledge and understanding.

The Cox Report (DES/WO 1989) took a mile marker approach to levels, treating them as minima (for example, para. 15.32) *except* in the case of level 1:

> We understand that level 1 is intended to encompass a wide range of attainment, from those pupils who have barely begun to learn, to those who are very close to level 2.
>
> (DES/WO 1989: para. 12.5)

This implies a broad (pathway) view of level 1, although, later in the same paragraph, the writers refer to children attaining level 1 as if, like other levels, it represents minima. This rather ambiguous position is illustrated diagrammatically in Figure 10.1(c).

With the exception of level 1, advice from SCAA, OFSTED and the DFE now seems to treat levels as broad stages (strictly speaking, encompassing an upwards gradient across the stage), rather than minima. The following extract from a letter to schools from OFSTED and SCAA implies that levels are to be regarded as broad stages. Deciding whether children have reached a particular level is thus an explicitly fuzzy judgement:

> In moving away from the detail of statements of attainment to level descriptions, we are looking to teachers to make a rounded judgement on which description best fits the overall performance of the individual child. There is no question of looking for an exact fit. Children may well be more advanced in one aspect of a subject than another, and it is, therefore, very much a matter for the teacher to decide which description best matches their overall performance.
>
> (SCAA/OFSTED 1994)

This emphasises the exercise of professional judgement and, by implication, the inevitable approximation in allocating a single level to areas of attainment. This suggests a weakening of an emphasis on criterion-referencing in National Curriculum attainment levels. A strictly criterion-referenced approach would take the lowest level achieved on any level descriptor in an attainment target to be the level attributable to the attainment target as a whole. The emphasis on exercising professional judgement also avoids some of the problems associated with aggregating a range of separate scores to produce a single score for an attainment target or subject (see Shorrocks et al. 1993 for an account of aggregation problems).

The anomalous position of level 1 at key stage 1 has the effect of introducing a comparatively strict criterion at that level. For children with learning difficulties this could have the effect of keeping them, for reporting and assessment purposes, at level W for a long time. This would be demoralising and inappropriate.

Differentiation by activity or by outcome

The three development agencies involved in piloting end of key stage assessments (CATS, NFER and STAIR) took different approaches. One difference between them was in whether they chose to use assessment tasks that differentiated children's attainments by activity or by outcome.

Differentiation by activity

Using differentiation by activity, children are designated as being at particular levels and given appropriate activities for their levels. This is crudely similar to dividing children in a class into ability groups and allocating work accordingly (red group do practical work, cutting up apples and labelling the parts; blue group do fractions workcards; green group do problems which involve using fractions, etc.). The Standard Tests and Assessment Implementation Research (STAIR) Consortium argued for differentiation by activity on the basis that the teacher's continuous assessment will alert her or him to the appropriate task for individual children. Thus, this makes the assessment build on the preceding teacher assessments. Differentiation by activity is embodied in the recommendation that at key stage 2, children who may be anxious, or perform badly in the standard tests, may carry out classroom-based tasks instead.

This is likely to draw attention to those children and the situation will need to be monitored closely if one set of potential disadvantages (being given tests which are inappropriate and perhaps demoralising) is not to be replaced by another set of disadvantages (being seen as receiving easier tasks and excluded from valued activities). More generally, teachers have been informed that they may adapt standard tests and tasks (at key stages 1 and 2) 'to reflect individual children's needs' (circular 21/94, pp. 12 and 22). Presumably this is an area that may receive particular attention from local authority- or SCAA-sponsored auditors.

For children who find school-based learning difficult, differentiation by activity may be more encouraging than differentiation by outcome. The children are not faced with activities outside their capabilities. However, this means that the children may be the victims of inappropriate teacher expectations; if the teacher does not anticipate that the child will succeed on an activity then the child will not get the chance to try it. This is less likely to happen if there have been good, continuous assessments of children's learning, although these would not prevent low expectations of a child.

Differentiation by outcome

Differentiation by outcome is illustrated in the activities which teachers often carry out with a new class, such as asking all of the children to swim from one side of a swimming pool to the other. As a result of watching all of the children do this same exercise, the teacher subdivides the class into 'non-swimmers', 'beginners', 'proficient swimmers', etc.

The TGAT Report (DES/WO 1988) recommended differentiation by outcome at key stage 1 and differentiation by activity, if necessary, at later key stages. Differentiation by outcome means that children who find learning difficult are not judged initially as being incapable of some tasks. All children have the same chance to show what they can do. Many activities could be curtailed when a child begins to have difficulties. However, to be faced repeatedly with activities which are too difficult is very demoralising and so differentiation by outcome requires very sensitive handling by teachers. This applies both before and after the tests, as it makes it easier for children to compare attainments and for classmates who have been unable to complete tests to feel 'shown up'. The NFER and CATS consortia based their developments of standard tests and tasks on differentiation by outcome.

Combining differentiation by activity and differentiation by outcome

In practice, standard tests and tasks could combine various sorts of differentiation. This could be done within an activity, whereby children might all have the same starting point but might then branch off into different activities depending on attainments on the first activity.

In the writing test in pilot key stage 2 material (1994) children had the same short story writing task although two starting points for the story were given. The choice of story opening (differentiation of interest) did not differentiate the task. Children were expected to write the story on their own (no differentiation of target task) and with a time limit (no differentiation of pace). However, the teacher could help with the planning of the story for children at levels 1 or 2 (differentiation of support at planning stage).

The reading test in the same series of materials allowed for greater differentiation, including differentiation by activity. In this test, based on a reading interview, the initial activity differed according to the level ascribed initially to the child by the teacher. At level 1 the teacher and child shared a book, and the teacher asked about, for example, individual words or letters. At level 2 the child read a passage from a book on the selected booklist. Children at levels 3–6 read a magazine, supplied with the test materials.

Age as the focus for timing of end of key stage assessments

The TGAT report (DES/WO 1988) advocated that age should be the basic criterion for deciding when a child should complete standard tasks. In other words, all 7-year-olds and all 11-year-olds (unless exempted through the statement of special educational needs or direction for temporary exceptions) should be carrying out standard tests and tasks regardless of either where they are likely to come on the ten (now eight + one) identified levels within each subject or how they are grouped for teaching. This has been modified in later documents to provide more flexibility, so that children can take the standard tests and tasks with their teaching groups rather than according to chronological ages. In general, standard tests and tasks are carried out when the majority of children in the teaching group are at the reporting ages (i.e. ages 7 and 11 in primary schools). So a 9-year-old in a teaching group with 7-year-olds for, say, English, would do standard tests and tasks on English at the same time as the 7-year-olds. Headteachers can use discretionary powers (see Chapter 11) to take such a child out of those assessment arrangements. In theory, if setting is used extensively across year groups, then a 9-year-old who is taught with 7-year-olds for English and with 6-year-olds for mathematics, would effectively receive a staggered ('little and often') statutory assessment programme across several years.

Moderation of assessments

Moderation of assessments of children with special needs now features in two complementary contexts – the National Curriculum and the Code of Practice (DFE 1994a).

Moderation of summative assessments on the National Curriculum was an important aspect of the TGAT Report (DES/WO 1988). Moderation, which focuses on the reliability as well as the validity of the assessment process, has been supplemented with auditing procedures (for key stage 1) which focus on the accuracy and reliability of reported summative assessments in the core subjects. DFE documents now refer to audit-moderation and verification, rather than moderation. Schools are encouraged to carry out an internal moderation procedure to 'ensure consistent standards' (circular 21/94, p. 9). At present, this is not statutory. Circular 21/94 suggests that moderation activities might include meetings of teachers within the school to scrutinise samples of children's work as well as similar meetings with teachers from other schools. The pattern will differ between key stages 1 and 2 because while external markers are to be used for standard tasks at key stage 2, key stage 1 tasks will be marked within the school.

At key stage 1 local education authorities are required to carry out an audit in order to verify assessment results in locally maintained schools. SCAA is to approve agencies to take a parallel role in grant-maintained schools. OFSTED (1993c) raised concerns about the variability in the ways in which the audit process was carried out.

A different sort of moderation is recommended in connection with the Code of Practice (DFE 1994a). The setting up of local authority moderation groups in order to support the consistent application of the Code is recommended by the DFE (DFE 1994g). These groups are seen as likely to involve headteachers. Focus is intended to be on patterns of assessments and statements across schools, rather than on discussion or scrutiny of individual cases. Although this has not been related to the moderation of National Curriculum assessments there may, in practice, be links between the two sets of procedures.

EVIDENCE FROM EXPERIENCE OF NATIONAL CURRICULUM SUMMATIVE ASSESSMENT PROCEDURES WITH CHILDREN WITH SPECIAL EDUCATIONAL NEEDS

Much has been written about standard tasks and, in particular, their use with children with special needs. The purpose of this section is to distil the main findings from a variety of evaluative research and critical commentaries. These findings relate mainly to key stage 1 as key stage 2 testing had been carried out in only a sample of pilot schools. It should be noted that the standard tests and tasks have varied from year to year. (See Bangs 1992, Bartlett and Peacey 1992, OFSTED 1993c, Reason 1993, Turner 1993, Lewis and Sammons 1994 for further data and discussion.)

- In general, SATs/standard tests and tasks were adapted satisfactorily for children with physical disabilities or for children with hearing/visual impairments.
- Children with emotional or behavioural difficulties tended to respond less well to the SATs/standard tests and tasks than did children with other kinds of special educational needs. In particular, children with emotional or behavioural difficulties sometimes had problems with group tasks.
- There was some evidence that teachers tended to underestimate the attainments of children with special needs. These children tended to obtain higher levels on SATs/standard tests and tasks than they did on parallel teacher assessments.
- The aggregation of assessments in SATs/standard tests and

tasks and the characteristics of the ten levels (in particular, the wide gap between levels 1 and 2 in some attainment targets) led to an under-representation of attainments of some children with special needs at level 1.

• The process of combining data to arrive at a SAT/standard tests and task level masked attainments, especially for children with learning difficulties, for whom small gains and/or uneven development needed to be emphasised.

• There was evidence of a neglect of children with special needs while SATs/standard tests and tasks were being given to other children. This is part of a broader and widely reported management problem concerning the neglect of 'non-SATs children' in mixed age classes. There were also repercussions across the school with support being deflected from non-SATs classes.

• Teachers went to great lengths to mediate the impact of SATs/standard tests and tasks, thereby compromising standardisation practices (Pollard et al. 1994).

• Support staff needed specific training in supporting children with special needs while those children were working on the SATs/standard tests and tasks.

• Pilot key stage 2 testing was 'usually undertaken under formal examination conditions' (OFSTED 1993c: 13). Reports that some special schools have used similar arrangements when administering summative assessment procedures with children with learning difficulties suggest that these schools were over-zealous in adhering to what their headteachers perceived as requirements (Lewis and Halpin 1994). 'Examination conditions' are likely to be very intimidating for anxious children and are particularly inappropriate for children with learning difficulties. OFSTED (1993c) noted that some children were reported as showing anxiety (further details not given).

Looking further ahead:

• The simplification of standard tests, with greater use of whole-class, pencil and paper tests at key stage 2 than at key stage 1, is likely to disadvantage children with reading, motivational and/or concentration problems. However the option of using classroom-based tasks instead of tests should alleviate these potential difficulties.

• There is pressure on resources for the modification of standard tests and tasks for children with hearing or visual impairments.

Dearing (NCC 1993c) expressed concerns about nationwide expertise in this area being stretched beyond capacity when both key stage 2 and key stage 3 tests/tasks are operating.

CARRYING OUT NATIONALLY PRESCRIBED ASSESSMENTS WITH CHILDREN WITH LEARNING DIFFICULTIES

If standard tests and tasks are a good way of measuring what they aim to assess (valid) and would give similar results from day to day or for different assessors (reliable), then they should be accepted as useful adjuncts to formative teacher assessments. Their major strength would be in enabling wider comparisons to be made between work in one school and broader standards. This would be valuable for several reasons.

Work on school effectiveness (for example, Mortimore *et al.* 1988, Tizard *et al.* 1988) has shown the wide differences between standards attained in schools in similar areas. In particular, it has been claimed that teachers often underestimate children with learning difficulties, whether those children are in mainstream or special schools (for example, Bennett *et al.* 1984). It would be useful for teachers and others to know if, for example, expectations for scientific understanding were low when compared with schools having similar populations. Similarly, it would be encouraging to know that reading levels, for example, compared well with schools in similar areas.

One of the factors which might lead children with learning difficulties to 'under-achieve' on standard tests and tasks, and so to produce an invalid assessment, is the child's motivation. Those children are likely to feel more confident, and so do better, if given 'easy' activities to begin with. If the child does not want to carry out a test or task then any apparent level of attainment on this is likely to underestimate what he or she can do. Children who find school-based learning difficult are likely to feel anxious in situations which appear to be unusual learning contexts. Their fear of failing may lead them to avoid new learning experiences rather than treating them as a challenge. Consequently, for those children it will be vital that standard tasks are, as recommended in the TGAT Report (DES/WO 1988), consistent with usual classroom practice.

The child's failure to understand what is expected or required may also limit his or her attainments. Much research in developmental psychology has shown the importance of the context in which the task is presented. Ask a child if there is more or less liquid when water is transferred from a short, fat glass to a tall, thin glass and many young children will answer wrongly that the tall, thin glass holds more water. However, put that task into a meaningful context, such as transferring orange juice from a cracked, short, fat glass to an uncracked, tall, thin glass, and the child recognises that no change has taken place in the amount of liquid (Light *et al.* 1979). Children with learning difficulties may, through lack of confidence in learning, be particularly likely to be swayed by the irrelevant in contexts which lack 'common sense' for them.

The child's understanding of the wording of the task is also important. For example, if a child is given a set of objects and asked to 'Sort these into magnetic and non-magnetic materials', the child may be unable to do this because the word 'magnetic' is not understood. If the task is rephrased, to 'Sort the objects into things which stick to the magnet and things which don't stick to the magnet', this removes the lexical problem of whether or not the child understands 'magnetic' but it introduces a distracting element because of the ambiguity of 'stick to'. In primary classes, 'stick to' is probably used more often to refer specifically to gluing things than to mean 'attract'. Consequently, the child with learning difficulties, seeing that he or she has not been supplied with glue, may do nothing and so 'fail' the task. There is another source of ambiguity in the phrasing of the initial question above, that is in the use of the word 'materials'. Whereas many primary children would understand that this is a general term for a variety of things, the child with learning difficulties may interpret 'materials' very specifically as 'fabrics'. This may lead the child to sort the objects into those which do or do not contain fabric. Both of these examples reflect a lack of ability to generalise terms and this may impede a child with learning difficulties. However, confusion over 'sticking' and 'materials' would not necessarily mean that the child failed to understand magnetism. Other children, more attuned to classroom language, will probably interpret the instruction as intended by the teacher.

Work on teacher language (for example, Edwards and Westgate 1987) has shown how the subtle conventions of classroom discourse are different from talk found outside classrooms. For example, if a child gives an incorrect answer to a question, then teachers commonly repeat the question but without saying that the first answer is incorrect:

TEACHER   What day is it today, Sandy?
SANDY   Saturday
TEACHER   What day is it today, Nicky?
NICKY   Tuesday.
TEACHER   That's right, Tuesday. Swimming day.

Most children tune into these discourse conventions but many children with difficulties in learning may not do so. They are often more inclined to interpret what is happening at face value. For instance, in the above example, they may not realise for some while that 'Saturday' was the incorrect answer because there was no specific feedback telling Sandy that it was incorrect. Conversely, children may be too ready to accept the convention that a repeated question means that the first answer was incorrect (Edwards and Mercer 1987). This is particularly so for a child who lacks confidence in his or her learning:

TEACHER   Does the bag of shells weigh more than the marble?
RACHEL   Yes.
TEACHER   Does the bag of shells weigh more than the marble?
RACHEL   No.

Teachers carrying out formal assessment procedures may be likely to repeat a question in order to be sure that they have understood the child's intended answer. That, as in the above extract, may confuse a child who lacks confidence and lead the child to 'correct' a right answer. Thus, there are various conventions of classroom language which become very significant when translated into an assessment context. The children who have failed to understand the conventions are not just naïve members of the class but are also failing to do themselves justice on cognitive tasks.

The teacher's expectations may also limit a child's attainments. An extensive body of research has shown that children tend to work at the levels expected of them. Crudely, children labelled as 'slow learners' tend to behave in that way while children identified as high achievers live up to expectations. In the context of standard tasks this means that, in a wide range of subtle ways, the teacher may convey to the child that he or she is not expected to be able to carry out an activity. This includes giving the child a relatively short time in which to respond, allowing interruptions from other children, or not rephrasing questions. This is important in the context of assessment and the National Curriculum because many of the level descriptions are unclear and so judgements about attainments are open to bias by the assessor.

Children who have difficulties in school-based learning are often described as having short concentration spans. Some standard tasks have entailed detailed and sustained work over one period. Some children may do poorly in such a situation, not because they are unable to complete the task but because they tend to work in short bursts and attention wanders over a longer period. Conversely, some children may need a relatively long time to complete an activity. If standard tasks are untimed then the teacher can allow for this. How standard tasks are managed in the class as a whole will have a bearing on whether or not the teacher can accommodate this. Some children might do better if they can carry out prolonged standard tasks in a quiet area outside the classroom.

The child's relationship with the teacher who is giving the assessment task is also likely to influence how well the child does on that task. One finding to emerge from psychological work on interview techniques has been the growing realisation of the influence of interviewer characteristics on the responses elicited. People respond differently to interviewers whom they like or dislike, who are of the same or opposite sex to themselves, who come from similar or contrasting backgrounds and who are of the same or a different ethnic group. Similarly, children with learning difficulties are likely to respond in very different ways to different teachers. The implication for assessment through standard tasks is that, ideally, schools need to give the child the best chance by careful choice of the adult(s) with whom the child works. In practice, it may be that this will always be the class teacher but there may be a case for using a support teacher to work through standard tasks with specific children.

There is strong and increasing evidence of the effect of age on school attainments (for example, Mortimore *et al.* 1988, Tizard *et al.* 1988, Sammons *et al.* 1994). Summer-born children starting school in the autumn following their fifth birthdays have one year less in the infant school compared with autumn-born children who start school at the beginning of the term in which their fifth birthdays fall. This means that at the end of key stage 1 some children may have had only two years in school (one-third of their lives) while other children will have had three years (nearly half of their lives). The significance of this is evident from surveys showing that a disproportionate number of children with difficulties in learning are the younger (i.e. summer-born) children in a year group. These children are not really less able than their classmates but just younger. In theory, results on standard tasks could take this into account but it would require a complex standardisation of standard tasks (as happens for standardised reading tests which adjust raw scores for chronological age in years and months).

The significance (for schools and perhaps care-givers) of standard tasks will be greater than attainments on other, more routine, school tasks. Despite the emphasis in the TGAT Report (DES/WO 1988), and in most of the key stage 1 standard tasks, on making these tasks part of normal classroom activities, it seems probable that children will pick up from teachers the relative seriousness attached to the standard tasks. This could work in two ways: it might motivate some children but might increase anxiety for others (especially those with low academic self-esteem). Children with learning difficulties are likely to be in this latter group. Children who fail to note the significance of standard tasks may underachieve because they quickly give up, lose interest or just prefer to do something else.

CONCLUSION

This discussion has highlighted various ways in which standard tasks may be invalid and unreliable, particularly in relation to children with learning difficulties. Some of these problems can only be overcome in the design of the tasks, and their development should lead to greater validity and reliability. Other threats to validity and reliability may be overcome by the way in which the teacher carries out the activities. All of the factors which enhance motivation, such as where, when and with whom the activity is done, should be arranged to give the children the best chance of showing attainments. Many of the points which were made in Chapter 6, concerning helping children to gain access to the National Curriculum, apply here. For example, some children may need to be told instructions rather than reading them independently, or they may need more time for tasks than do other children.

This chapter was written in November 1994 and reflects the position at that time.

The discussion of threats to validity and reliability of results from standard tests and tasks should be set in the context of the limitations of the summative tests of children's attainments which were used prior to the National Curriculum. Many surveys attest to the widespread use of out-of-date standardised tests which have had little relationship to classroom teaching. There are, potentially, advantages in standard tests and tasks if these are planned and carried out sensitively within a broader assessment programme. It may be the case that teachers believe, even so, that children with difficulties in learning are not doing themselves justice in terms of attainments on standard tasks. If this is the case then it is important to collate the associated evidence so that the assessment process can continue to be modified accordingly.

Chapter 11

Formal modifications and disapplications of the National Curriculum

The emphasis in the National Curriculum is that it is for all children in maintained schools (with the single exception of the small group of children in hospital special schools). It is not enough to have the National Curriculum available generally in a school. The National Curriculum, as described in the Orders, must be offered to every child in maintained schools unless modifications or disapplications have been made.

Given that this is the statutory position, one may ask 'Is it desirable that children with learning difficulties are, in principle, to be included in the National Curriculum?' If the answer to this question is 'yes', then discussion of modifications and disapplications will focus on how to minimise these. However, as Jean Ware (1990) has argued (in relation to children with severe learning difficulties) it is conceivable that it would benefit children to be exempted, or freed, from the National Curriculum. In that case, discussion might focus on how to maximise disapplications and modifications. The stance taken in this book is that full participation in the National Curriculum is a desirable, initial goal for all children in mainstream schools.

There are many ways in which the National Curriculum might be adapted, for example, through helping children to gain access to the curriculum (discussed in Chapters 5 and 6) or placing the child in a teaching group with younger children (see Chapter 7). These ways are informal and do not require formal modifications. Such informal modifications slide into formal modifications and it is not clear when the former become the latter (Daniels and Ware 1990). Formal modifications or disapplications of the National Curriculum may be used in various situations, not exclusively for children with difficulties in learning.

PROCEDURES FOR FORMALLY MODIFYING OR DISAPPLYING THE NATIONAL CURRICULUM

There are five routes through which the National Curriculum may be modified or disapplied and these may be related to: children with statements of special educational needs; children with special educational needs who do not have statements; children who, through special circumstances such as prolonged illness, may none the less not receive the National Curriculum for a period of time (nominally up to six months); children, not necessarily having special educational needs, who are involved in development work.

'Disapplication' means that the child is not involved in specified parts of the National Curriculum. 'Modification' means that the National Curriculum, although the child will be following it, is altered in some way (see Norwich 1989). The need for individual modification has diminished substantially as a result of revisions to the National Curriculum. For example, work outside the key stage is now permissible. This means that, for example, at key stage 2 children may carry out level 1 work without this requiring a formal modification of the child's statement of special educational needs. Similarly, the National Curriculum now contains frequent references to children using signing systems to access or demonstrate aspects of attainment targets. So these too do not require formal modification of a statement.

1 Disapplication through a statement of special educational needs

There are four main elements in the National Curriculum: subjects, programmes of study, attainment targets and assessment arrangements. A child's statement could specify disapplication (or modification) of any one or more of these aspects (1988 Education Act, section 18). For example, a child might be exempted from certain foundation subjects in order to give more curriculum time for self-help skills. Alternatively, a child might follow all foundation subjects but not all attainment targets. This is possible although, in practice, unlikely. It would also be possible, although this is being discouraged, for a statement to disapply only part of the assessment arrangements; for example, to indicate that a child should follow all of the programmes of study and attainment targets in science but should not be included in standard assessment tests or tasks. At key stage 2 a child can be exempted from standard tests without recourse to a formal procedure. Circular 21/94 (DFE 1994f) implies that this is possible without any formal disapplication because such legitimate variation in assessment procedures will reflect teachers' professional judgements (see Chapter 10). Numbers of children involved in disapplication, or modification, of the National Curriculum through statements of special educational needs are small. Six per cent (disapplication through statement) and 11 per cent (modification through statement) of mainstream primary schools (Lewis 1995a) reported using these strategies. Interestingly, primary schools with a designated governor for special needs issues made more use of modifications (but not disapplication) than did other schools (Lewis 1995a). Unravelling the causal relationships here requires further research.

Any disapplication in a child's statement of special educational needs must be accompanied by an account of what is to be offered as an alternative, bearing in mind that all pupils should receive a broad and balanced curriculum (DES 1989g). This leaves unanswered questions about what would be permissible within the 1988 and 1993 Education Acts. Children with emotional and behavioural difficulties might need a curriculum heavily oriented to developing personal and social skills although, in the terms expressed in the 1988 Education Act, this would break the statutory requirement for a broad and balanced curriculum.

2 Disapplication through a temporary 'direction'

A headteacher may temporarily disapply the National Curriculum for a child for, initially, up to six months (1988 Education Act, section 19). Temporary exceptions ('directions') are of two kinds: general directions and special directions. The associated 1989 regulations (DES 1989g) have not been rescinded or amended through the provisions of the 1993 Education Act or revisions to the National Curriculum (DFE 1994h). There is little published evidence about the extent to which general directions and special directions have been used. One survey (Lewis 1995a) found that 14 per cent of mainstream primary schools reported taking small numbers of children out of the National Curriculum 'informally'. This may have included the use of directions.

General directions

General directions can be applied in a diverse range of circumstances including: pupils newly arrived from a different education system; pupils who have had some time in hospital, who have been educated at home or been excluded from school; pupils who temporarily have severe emotional problems; children who, for reasons other than these, have had extended absence from school (DES 1989g: para. 13). A headteacher does not have to make general directions in these circumstances. General directions can also be given for a child who has a statement of special educational needs.

There are several categories for which general directions are not needed. These categories include: children away from school through illness or holidays, children who have been temporarily excluded from school, children concentrating for several weeks on areas in which they have particular weaknesses and children who are on the register of a school but receive part of their education elsewhere (DES 1989g).

The groups of children included in these two sets of categories are extremely confusing and it is difficult to envisage how these general directions can operate consistently and effectively in practice. There seems to be little logic in which groups may or may not be the subject of directions.

Special directions

The other category of temporary exceptions ('special directions') applies to children to cover the period during which they are 'being assessed for special educational needs' or statements of special educational needs are being prepared (DES 1989g: para. 19).

Procedures

The procedures for applying special directions are similar to the procedures for general directions and are summarised in Table 11.1. Directions have to be made for individual pupils, not groups so that a group direction could not be made, for example, on all of the children receiving extra reading support. Before giving a

Table 11.1 Summary table of procedures for making an initial direction

Schools	General directions	Special directions
LEA maintained		
Recommended consultation with:	Parents[1] Teachers Specialists	Parents[1] Teachers Specialists
Required consultation with:		LEA
Prior written consent in case if renewal from:	3 governors[2] LEA[3]	
Prior written consent in case of new direction[4] from:	LEA	3 governors LEA
Inform (in writing):	Parents[1] Chair of governors LEA	Parents[1] Chair of governors LEA
Grant-maintained		
Recommended consultation with	Parents[1] Teachers Specialists	Parents[1] Teachers Specialists
Required consultation with:		LEA
Prior written consent in case of renewal from:	3 governors[2] LEA[2]	
Prior written consent in case of new direction[4] from:	3 governors	3 governors
Inform (in writing):	Parents[1] Chair of governors	Parents[1] Chair of governors LEA

[1] 'Parents' denotes at least one parent or guardian of the child, as registered at the school.
[2] if first and second renewal.
[3] Second renewal.
[4] Must be based on different reasons from previous direction.
Source: Regulations (1981, 1989) and accompanying Circular 15/89 (DES 1989g)

direction it is *expected* that the headteacher will *consult*: the class teacher, the child's parent(s)/guardian(s), and specialist staff such as educational psychologists and medical officers. This consultation is expected, but not mandatory, and this has been criticised as diminishing the importance of, in particular, liaison with parents (Russell 1990). Once a general or special direction has been made, the headteacher must, within three working days, inform in writing: at least one of the child's parent(s)/guardian(s) (as registered at the school), the chair of the school governing body and the local education authority (if the school is local education authority maintained). Where the parents or guardians have difficulty in understanding a direction, the headteacher should make appropriate arrangements to explain what is planned; for example, by providing a translation (written or oral) of the direction.

The headteacher must generally allow one month before the direction comes into force, although in exceptional cases it can be brought in more quickly. This is to give parents and the local education authority (for schools maintained by the local education authority) time to query the proposed direction. The direction must include the following information: which type of direction is being applied, why the action is being taken, what type of action is being taken, and what alternatives to the National Curriculum are being offered (these must be 'positive alternatives'). In addition, for a general direction, the headteacher must specify: why present circumstances prevent the child from receiving the National Curriculum, how these circumstances seem likely to change over the period of the direction (i.e. the next six months [or less]), and how the child will be brought back into the National Curriculum. If a child who is the subject of a general or special direction leaves the school, then the direction ceases to apply. The headteacher of the child's new school would have to decide whether or not a new direction is needed. Directions can be transferred from one head-teacher of a school to his or her successor.

Varying or revoking a direction

If a general direction has been brought in because, for example, a child has been in hospital, this direction might well be nominally for six months (it could be for a shorter period). However, if after, say, three months it is decided that there is no need for the direction to continue then the headteacher could revoke or change the direction. The procedures for informing relevant individuals of an initial direction apply again when giving information about changing or withdrawing the direction.

One possible type of variation of a direction within a six monthly period would be for a child attending a unit away from the school for a short period. For example, a general direction might be used to enable a child to attend a reading support unit in an local education authority centre for two terms (for example, January–June) but one term might turn out to be sufficient or, because of pressure on unit places, the child attends for only one term. Then the headteacher would have to amend the initial direction to show that the child returned to the home school full-time after (say) three, not six months. If the headteacher with-draws a direction then he or she must state the reasons for this, when it is to take effect and how the child is to be reintegrated into the National Curriculum.

Renewing directions

General directions can be renewed by the head, firstly for a further three months (provided that written consent is obtained from three school governors). The renewal has to follow the initial direction, so that a headteacher could not bring in a temporary direction for (for example) January–June, let it lapse over July–August and then 'renew' the initial direction in September. A second renewal of the initial direction is possible for a further three months, so that heads can, in effect, bring in a temporary exemption from the National Curriculum for twelve months. However, the second three-monthly renewal has to be agreed both with three school governors and (for local education authority maintained schools) with the local education authority. A broadly similar situation applies to renewing special directions. In all types of renewals of directions, the same consultative processes as were outlined when making the initial direction are expected to take place.

A headteacher cannot bring in any further general directions for an individual child after this maximum twelve-month direction unless different reasons are given. Thus it would be possible to make general directions disapplying or modifying the National Curriculum for up to twelve months on the basis of a child's learning difficulties and then bring in a new set of directions based on the child's emotional difficulties. Making a second direction on a child requires prior written consent of three school governors and (for schools maintained by the local education authority) the local education authority.

The system, while apparently trying to meet the possible needs of individual children, is open to abuse. The misuse of temporary exceptions, for example, a casual and excessive use of them in order to remove 'difficult' children from the system, was recognised by the Department of Education and Science. Amendments to the draft circular on temporary exceptions were made in order to 'lay added emphasis on the intention that the powers of direction should be used sparingly' and it was stated that, 'the Secretary of State will be monitoring the powers of direction' (DES 1989g: annex A). It is not clear what action would be taken, or by whom, against a school which appeared to be 'over-applying' directions.

3 Orders issued by the Secretary of State

Orders have been made by the Secretary of State under section 4 of the 1988 Education Act to disapply or modify the National Curriculum for certain groups of children. The Orders for some of the individual subjects include amended attainment targets for children with specific types of learning difficulties.

4 Regulations issued by the Secretary of State

Groups of children with learning difficulties, with or without statements, may also be exempt from the National Curriculum through regulations issued by the Secretary of State (1988 Education Act, section 17). It would be feasible for, say, children with severe learning difficulties to be exempted from (for example) a foreign language by means of group regulations, although to date no such regulations have been applied to children with learning difficulties. Klaus Wedell (1990) reported only one instance of these regulations and this was in relation to pupils who attained level 10 before age 16.

5 Exemption from National Curriculum through development work

The 1988 Education Act (section 16) specifies that children in a particular school may have the National Curriculum disapplied or modified for development work or experiments to be carried out.

PARENTS' RIGHTS CONCERNING FORMAL MODIFICATIONS AND DISAPPLICATIONS

Parents (or guardians) can make a request, initially to the head-teacher and then to the school governors, that the National

Curriculum (and/or associated assessment arrangements) be disapplied or modified for their child. Similarly, parents can request that a disapplication or modification be changed and that their child be brought back into the National Curriculum. Parents do not have the power to remove their child from the National Curriculum while the child is educated within the state system. Parental concerns about the National Curriculum have tended to be directed, in particular, at summative assessment arrangements. Parental opposition to standard tests 'would not in itself constitute sufficient ground for [such] a direction' and 'It would not be appropriate to modify or disapply the assessment arrangements simply because parents report that the child would find them stressful' (DFE 1994f: paras 26, 28).

It is preferable if such requests can be discussed and resolved informally between the headteacher and the parents but regulations on temporary exemptions from the National Curriculum (DES 1989g) lay down very specific procedures if informal discussions do not resolve the issue. In this situation, parents must then put their request in writing to the headteacher. The headteacher has to consider changing a direction once only during the course of that direction, so that parents could, for example, expect a reply from their first request that one six-monthly direction be changed. However, if the parents continued to ask for this (for example, every month), then the headteacher would not be bound by law to reply to these subsequent requests. Similarly, the headteacher has to reply to only one such request during any one renewal.

Once the written request has been made by the parents, the headteacher must reply within two weeks. If the headteacher disagrees with the parents' request, then the headteacher has to write to the parents, to the governing body and (if a local education authority maintained school) to the local education authority, explaining his or her reasons. If the headteacher agrees with the parents then clearly appropriate action is set in motion. If the parents do not hear from the headteacher in writing within two weeks of their request, or if the headteacher turns it down, then the parents can take the request to the governing body. Circular 15/89 on temporary exceptions advises that governors should deal 'with all due speed' (DES 1989g: para. 6, annex B) with such appeals. To help governors to respond quickly to parental requests concerning the National Curriculum, any member of the governing body (except the headteacher) or any committee of governors can hear the appeal. The governors have three options. They can decide to agree with the headteacher, agree with the parents, or 'take any other action they consider appropriate within the scope of the regulations' (DES 1989g: para. 8, annex B). The headteacher must comply with the governors' decision.

These procedures place a lot of power in the hands of possibly inexperienced governors and have implications for governor training in local education authorities. They also make the role of the special educational needs coordinator very important, in relation to informing and advising school governors about special needs work and resources in the school (see Chapter 8). Regulations concerning parental appeals under the 1981 and 1993 Education Acts remain and are slightly strengthened as parents must now be informed in writing of any revision to a child's statement.

CONCLUSION

This chapter has reviewed formal procedures for disapplying or modifying the National Curriculum. The statutory mechanisms sit uneasily alongside the rhetoric of the National Curriculum which stresses its suitability for all children. If the National Curriculum is really attuned to individuals' learning needs then there should be no cause for any disapplications or modifications. Revisions to the National Curriculum can be seen as making it more flexible and so less likely to invoke exemption procedures.

Endnote
Continuity, direction and connectivity

Charles Handy (1994), in his writing on management and organisation theory, identifies three fundamental needs: continuity, direction and connectivity. He argues that successful organisations and societies meet those needs. Similar themes recur in the writing of a wide range of social commentators, psychologists and philosophers (see, for example, the work of Alvin Toffler and Dorothy Rowe). One approach to exploring the impact of the National Curriculum is to consider how well it seems to address those needs.

Continuity

The National Curriculum is part of an evolving curriculum. It reflects continuity as it is both a product of what went before and a force which shapes what is to follow. It is thus important to continue to collect systematic evidence about the impact of the National Curriculum on children with special needs. It is from this evidence that the effects of that curriculum must be judged. The implementation of the Code of Practice should help in this process. It incorporates tight monitoring of learning targets through (from stage 2) individual education plans and if these are linked to National Curriculum targets then monitoring of the child's learning is also a monitoring of the curriculum.

The evidence about the impact of the National Curriculum on children with special educational needs should monitor processes as well as outcomes. There continues to be a need for debate and analysis about ways of teaching the National Curriculum to children with special needs. Many special schools have retained the centrality of the cross-curricular elements as ways of teaching the National Curriculum and their work provides an interesting contrast to approaches taken in most primary schools. As we do not know, perhaps cannot know, which strategies will be most effective there is a good case for fostering pluralism in teaching methods.

It seems likely that the government's five-year moratorium on changes to the content of the National Curriculum will encourage focus on how that curriculum is being implemented. Once curricular content is seen as fixed, it is logical that attention will turn to how that content is being taught and learned.

Sense of direction

The National Curriculum has also provided a powerful sense of direction. Whether one agrees with the line of that direction is another issue. A sense of direction provides a marker against which to judge where we are going and want to go. In this connection, the use made of non-National Curriculum time for children with special needs should be monitored and evaluated. The use made of non-National Curriculum time will reflect teachers' educational priorities or pressures. So by looking carefully at the focus, for children with special educational needs, of work outside the National Curriculum we may become clearer about the perceived purposes of education for those children.

Connectivity

The visibility (whether reflecting perceived positive or negative features) of the National Curriculum is impressive. SCAA (1994a) reported that in a 1994 Gallup survey only 6 per cent of the 1,060 adults questioned had not heard of the National Curriculum.

The National Curriculum, like it or loathe it, has provided a common platform for debate among a wide range of professionals, parents and school governors. It has linked teachers across age phases, across special and mainstream schools and across countries. The National Curriculum is taught over a wide geographical area. Respondents to a survey about the National Curriculum included teachers in British Forces and International schools from around the world (Lewis 1995a).

The introduction of the National Curriculum has also given pupils a sense of being part of a shared educational structure.

Pupils in special schools have reported positive feelings about doing 'the same work' as friends and neighbours in mainstream schools (Costley, in preparation). For example, 15- and 16-year olds from schools for pupils with moderate learning difficulties could not outline what the National Curriculum was but when this was explained to them they responded with comments like: 'It's good because everybody does the same thing in each school; 'It's good because everyone wants to be equal'; and 'It makes it easier if everyone's doing the same thing, if you want to move from this school to another school.'

Looking further ahead this common curricular currency has the potential for, having linked the language, stronger linking of resources, provision and expertise. The National Council for Educational Technology is running a study in which special needs coordinators are linked, via electronic mail, to one another and to key sources of special needs expertise. It is possible to imagine a school system in which technological developments encourage a highly coordinated and responsive structure of geographically dispersed, perhaps small-scale, provision.

The National Curriculum has met needs for continuity, direction and connectivity in education. Now teachers have to shape the teaching and learning of that curriculum in ways which work to the benefit of all children. I have a friend who says that boulders may be stepping stones or stumbling blocks. Boulders are, in themselves, neutral. It is the way in which we respond to them that turns them into stepping stones or stumbling blocks. It is a tribute to teachers' professionalism and enthusiasm that they have in the main treated the National Curriculum as a stepping stone rather than a stumbling block.

Bibliography

Adams, M.J. (1990) *Beginning to Read: Thinking and Learning about Print*, Cambridge, Mass.: MIT Press.

Ainscow, M. and Muncey, J. (1984) *Special Needs Action Programme (SNAP)*, Cardiff: Drake/Coventry Local Education Authority.

Ainscow, M. and Tweddle, D. (1979) *Preventing Classroom Failure: An Objectives Approach*, London: Wiley.

Ainscow, M. and Tweddle, D. (1984) *Early Learning Skills Analysis* (ELSA), London: Wiley.

Alexander, R.J., Rose, J. and Woodhead, C. (1992) *Curriculum Organisation and Classroom Practice in Primary Schools: A Discussion Paper*, London: DES.

Alexander, R.J., Willcocks, J. and Kinder, K. (1989) *Changing Primary Practice*, Lewes: Falmer.

Allen, V.L. (1976) *Children as Teachers*, New York: Academic Press.

Alston, J. and Taylor, J. (1987) *Handwriting: Theory, Research and Practice*, London: Croom Helm.

Archer, M. (1989) 'Targeting change', *Special Children* 33, 14–15.

Arnold, H. (1982) *Listening to Children Reading*, London: Hodder and Stoughton/UKRA.

Ashdown, R., Carpenter, B. and Bovair, K. (eds) (1991) *The Curriculum Challenge: Pupils with Severe Learning Difficulties and the National Curriculum*, Lewes: Falmer.

Ashman, A.F. and Conway, R.N.F. (1989) *Cognitive Strategies for Special Education*, London: Routledge.

ATL (Association of Teachers and Lecturers) (1994) *Achievement for All*, London: ATL.

Aubrey, C. (1993) 'The primacy of pedagogy', *Special Children* 70, 14–17.

Audit Commission (1994) *The Act Moves on: Progress in Special Educational Needs*, London: HMSO.

Audit Commission/HMI (1992) *Getting in on the Act*, London: HMSO.

Avann, P. (1985) *Teaching Information Skills in the Primary School*, London: Arnold.

AVP (1992) *Special Needs: Computer Software and Resources*, Chepstow: AVP.

Bangs, J. (1992) 'And reactions from special schools', *British Journal of Special Education* 19: 3, 98–9.

Bannon, M., Wildig, C. and Jones, P.W. (1992) 'Teachers' perceptions of epilepsy', *Archives of Disease in Childhood* 67, 1467–71.

Barsby, J. (1991) 'Self-evaluation and seven year olds', *Education 3–13* 19: 1, 12–17.

Bartlett, D. and Peacey, N. (1992) 'Assessments – and issues – for 1992', *British Journal of Special Education* 19: 3, 94–7

Bastiani, J. (ed.) (1987) *Parents and Teachers 1: Perspectives on Home–School Relations*, Windsor: NFER/Nelson.

Beard, R. (1987) *Developing Reading 3–13*, London: Hodder and Stoughton.

Beck, K. (1989) 'Parental involvement in school: some dilemmas', *Education 3–13* 17: 3 10–13.

Beech, J.R. and Harding, L. (eds) (1991) *Educational Assessment in the Primary School*, Windsor: NFER/Nelson.

Bell, G.H. and Colbeck, B. (1989) *Experiencing Integration: The Sunnyside Action Enquiry Project*, Lewes: Falmer.

Bennett, N. (1990) 'Cooperative learning in classrooms: processes and outcomes', *Journal of Child Psychology and Psychiatry* 32: 4, 581–94.

Bennett, N. and Cass, A. (1988) 'The effects of group composition on group interactive processes and pupil understanding', *British Educational Research Journal* 19: 2, 121–32.

Bennett, N. and Cass, A. (1989) *From Special to Ordinary Schools: Case Studies in Integration*, London: Cassell.

Bennett, N. and Kell, A. (1989) *A Good Start?*, Oxford: Blackwell.

Bennett, N., Desforges, C., Cockburn, A. and Wilkinson, B. (1984) *The Quality of Pupil Learning Experiences*, London: Lawrence Erlbaum Associates.

Biott, C. and Easen, P. (1994) *Collaborative Learning in Staffrooms and Classrooms*, London: Fulton.

Blatchford, P. (1989) *Playtime in the Primary School*, Windsor: NFER/Nelson.

Blatchford, P. and Cline, T. (1992) 'Baseline assessment for school entrants', *Research Papers in Education* 7: 3, 247–69.

Blyth, C.A. and Wallace, F.M.S. (1988) 'An investigation into the difficulties of transferring written records from the nursery school to the primary school', *Educational Research* 30: 3, 219–23.

Bostock, A., Cooppan, A., O'Reilly, W., Perry, L. and Swapp, J. (1990) *The Real Reading Analysis*, Cambridge: LDA.

Bruce, T. (1987) *Early Childhood Education*, London: Hodder and Stoughton.

CACE (1967) *Children and their Primary Schools*, London: HMSO.

Calderhead, J. (ed.) 1988) *Teachers' Professional Learning*, Lewes: Falmer.

Campbell, J. and Emery, H. (1994) 'Curriculum policy for key stage 2: possibilities, contradictions and constraints', pp. 9–22 in H. Pollard (ed.) *Look Before You Leap: Research Evidence for the Curriculum at Key Stage 2*, London: Tufnell Press.

Campbell, R.J. and Neill, S.R. St J. (1994) *Primary Teachers at Work*, London: Routledge.

Carpenter, B. and Lewis, A. (1989) 'Searching for solutions: a curriculum for integration of SLD and PMLD children', pp. 103–24 in D. Baker and K. Bovair (eds) *Making the Special Schools Ordinary?*, Lewes: Falmer.

Carpenter, B., Fathers, J., Lewis, A. and Privett, R. (1988) 'Integration: the Coleshill experience', *British Journal of Special Education* 15: 3, 119–21.

Christie, T. (1990) 'Address to the National Primary Conference', Scarborough, reported in *Junior Education*, 9 June.

Clark, M.M., Barr, J.E. and Dewhirst, W. (1984) *Early Education of Children with Communication Problems: particularly those from ethnic minorities*, Offset publication no. 3, Birmingham: University of Birmingham.

Cleave, S., Jowett, S. and Bate, M. (1982) *And So to School*, Windsor: NFER/Nelson.

Cline, T. and Blatchford, P. (1994) 'Baseline assessment: selecting a method of assessing children on school entry', *Education 3–13* 22: 3, 10–15.

Coopers and Lybrand Deloitte (1991) *Costs of the National Curriculum in Primary Schools*, London: NUT.

Costley, D. (1994) 'All change', *Special Children* 74, 20–2.

Costley, D. (in preparation) 'The impact of the National Curriculum for pupils with moderate learning difficulties at key stage 4', University of Warwick.

Coventry LEA (1992) 'Small steps in English and mathematics' (draft) Coventry, Special Needs Suppport Team: Coventry LEA.

Crocker, A.C. and Cheeseman, R.G. (1988) 'The ability of young children to rank themselves for academic ability', *Educational Studies* 14: 1, 105–10.

Croft, P. (1989) 'The practice papers: resourcing the curriculum', *Special Children* 34, 1–4 November.

Croll, P. (1986) *Systematic Classroom Observation*, Lewes: Falmer.

Croll, P. and Moses, D. (1985) *One in Five*, London: Routledge.

Cronbach, L.J. and Snow, R.E. (1977) *Abilities and Instructional Methods*, New York: Irvington.

Daniels, H. and Ware, J. (1990) (eds) *Special Educational Needs and the National Curriculum*, Bedford Way Series, London: Kogan Page/Institute of Education, University of London.

Daniels, H., Norwich, B. and Anghileri, N. (1993) 'Teacher support teams: an evaluation of a school-based approach to meeting special educational needs', *Support for Learning* 8: 4, 169–73.

Darnbrough, A. and Kinrade, D. (1985) *Directory for Disabled People*, 4th edn, London: RADAR/Woodhead-Faulkner.

David, T. and Lewis, A. (1991) 'Assessment in the reception class', pp. 13–26 in J.R. Beech and L. Harding (eds) *Educational Assessment in the Primary School*, Windsor: NFER/Nelson.

Dawson, R. (1985) *TIPS*, London: Macmillan Education.

DES (1978a) *Primary Education in England*, London: HMSO.

DES (1978b) *Special Educational Needs* (Warnock Report), London: HMSO.

DES (1982a) *Education 5 to 9*, London: HMSO.

DES (1982b) *Mathematics Counts* (Cockcroft Report), London: HMSO.

DES (1985) *The Curriculum from 5–16*, Curriculum Matters 2 (HMI series), London: HMSO.

DES (1987a) *Primary School Staffing Survey*, London: DES.

DES (1987b) *The National Curriculum 5–16: A Consultation Document*, London: DES.

DES (1988) *The New Teacher in School*, London: HMSO.

DES (1989a) *A Survey of Pupils with Special Educational Needs in Ordinary Schools*, A report by HMI, London: DES.

DES (1989b) *The Education Reform Act 1988: The School Curriculum and Assessment*, Circular 5/89, London: HMSO.

DES (1989c) *The Implementation of the National Curriculum in Primary Schools*, HMI report, London: DES.

DES (1989d) *The Education Reform Act 1988: National Curriculum: Mathematics and Science Orders under Section 4,* Circular 6/89, London: HMSO.

DES (1989e) *Assessments and Statements of Special Educational Needs: Procedures within the Education, Health and Social Services*, Circular 22/89, London: HMSO.

DES (1889f) *From Policy to Practice*, London: DES.

DES (1989g) *The Education Reform Act 1988: Temporary Exceptions from the National Curriculum*, Circular 15/89, London: HMSO.

DES (1989h) *A Survey of Support Services for Special Educational Needs*, HMI report, London: DES.

DES (1990a) *Education Observed: Special Needs Issues*, A report by HMI, London: HMSO.

DES (1990b) *The Education Reform Act 1988: National Curriculum: English Stages Two to Four Order under Section 4*, Circular 2/90, London: HMSO.

DES (1990c) *Standards in Education. A Report by HMI*, London: DES.

DES (1990d) *Provision for Primary aged Pupils with Statements of Special Educational Needs in Mainstream Schools*, HMI report, London: DES.

DES (1990e) *The Education Reform Act 1988: National Curriculum Section 4 Order; Technology: Design and Technology and Information Technology*, Circular 3/90, London: HMSO.

DES (1990f) *Records of Achievement*, Circular 8/90, London: HMSO.

DES (1990g) *The Implementation of the National Curriculum in Primary Schools: A Survey of 100 Schools*, HMI report, London: DES.

DES (1990h) *The Education Reform Act 1988: The Education (National Curriculum) (Assessment Arrangements for English, Mathematics and Science) Order 1990*, Circular 9/90, London: HMSO.

DES (1991a) *National Curriculum and Special Needs 1989–90*, A report by HMI, London: HMSO.

DES (1991b) *The Work and Professional Development of Advisory Teachers for Special Educational Needs*, A report by HMI, London: DES.

DES/WO (1988) *National Curriculum: Task Group on Assessment and Testing* (TGAT Report), London: HMSO.

DES/WO (1989) *English for ages 5 to 16* (Cox Report), London: HMSO.

DFE (1993) *The Education (National Curriculum) (Assessment Arrangements for the Core Subjects) (Key Stage 1) Order*, Circular 11/93 (NB: superseded by circular 21/94), London: DFE.

DFE (1994a) *Code of Practice on the Identification and Assessment of Special Educational Needs*, London: DFE.

DFE (1994b) *Exclusions from School*, Circular 10/94, London: DFE.

DFE (1994c) *Education (School Information) (England) Regulations*, London: DFE.

DFE (1994d) *The Parent's Charter: Publication of Information about Primary Schools in 1994*, Circular 15/94, London: DFE.

DFE (1994e) *Special Educational Needs: A Guide for Parents*, London: DFE.

DFE (1994f) *Assessing 7 and 11 year olds in 1995*, Circular 21/94, London: DFE.

DFE (1994g) *The Organisation of Special Educational Provision*, Circular 6/94, London: DFE.

DFE (1994h) Personal communication.

DFE (1995) *The National Curriculum*, London: HMSO.

Dunne, E. and Bennett, N. (1990) *Talking and Learning in Groups*, London: Macmillan.

Dussart, G. (1994) 'Identifying the clumsy child in school: an exploratory study', *British Journal of Special Education* 21: 2, 81–6.

Edwards, A.D. and Westgate, D.P.G. (1987) *Investigating Classroom Talk*, Lewes: Falmer.

Edwards, D. and Mercer, N. (1987) *Common Knowledge*, London: Methuen.

Elbaz, F. (1983) *Teacher Thinking: A Study of Practical Knowledge*, New York: Nichols.

Elliot, S., Mills, G., Stephenson, P. and Underwood, H. (1992) *Differentiation: An INSET Training Package*, Lewes: East Sussex County Council.

Evans, L. (1990) 'Small steps to success: resource pack', *Special Children* 35, 2–5 (inset).

Fagg, S., Aherne, P., Skelton, S. and Thornber, A. (1990) *Entitlement for All in Practice*, London: David Fulton.

Fletcher-Campbell, F. (with Hall, C.) (1993) *LEA Support for Special Needs*, Windsor: NFER-Nelson.

Fletcher-Campbell, F. (1994) *Still Joining Forces?*, Slough: NFER.

Flude, M. and Hammer, M. (eds) (1990) *The Education Reform Act 1988: Its Origins and Implications*, Lewes: Falmer.

Fox, G. (1993) *A Handbook for Special Needs Assistants: Working in Partnership with Teachers*, London: David Fulton.

Gagné, R.M. (1968) 'Learning hierarchies', *Educational Psychology* 6: 1, 3–6.

Galton, M. and Williamson, J. (1992) *Group Work in the Primary Classroom*, London: Routledge.

Galton, M., Simon, B. and Croll, P. (1980) *Inside the Primary Classroom*, London: Routledge.

Garner, M., Petrie, I. and Pointon, D. (1991) *LEA Support Services for Meeting Special Educational Needs*, Stafford: SENNAC (SEN National Advisory Council).

Gipps, C. (1994) 'Teacher assessment and teacher development in primary schools', Address to the annual conference of the Association for the Study of Primary Education (ASPE), Hertfordshire, September.

Gipps, C. and Murphy, P. (1994) *A Fair Test?*, Milton Keynes: Open University.

Gipps, C. and Stobart, G. (1993) *Assessment: A Teacher's Guide to the Issues*, London: Hodder and Stoughton.

Gipps, C., Gross, H. and Goldstein, H. (1987) *Warnockl's Eighteen Per Cent: Children with Special Needs in Primary Schools*, Lewes: Falmer.

Glynn, T. (1985) 'Contexts for independent learning', *Educational Psychology* 5: 1, 5–15.

Goacher, B., Evans, J., Welton, J. and Wedell, K. (1988) *Policy and Provision for Special Educational Needs*, London: Cassell.

Graham, D. (with Tytler, D.) (1993a) *A Lesson for Us All*, London: Routledge.

Graham D. (1993b) 'Reflections on the first four years', pp. 2–9 in M. Barber and D. Graham, *Sense, Nonsense and the National Curriculum*, Lewes: Falmer.

Gross, J. (1993) *Special Educational Needs in the Primary School*, Buckingham: Open University Press.

Gurney, P. (1990) 'The enhancement of self-esteem in junior classrooms', pp. 7–24 in J. Docking (ed.) *Education and Alienation in the Junior School*, Lewes: Falmer.

Handy, C. (1994) *The Empty Raincoat*, London: Hutchinson.

Hanko, G. (1985) *Special Needs in Ordinary Classrooms*, Oxford: Blackwell.

Haring, N.G., Lovitt, T.C., Eaton, M.D. and Hansen, C.L. (1978) *The Fourth R: Research in the Classroom*, Columbus, OH: Merrill.

Hastings, N. and Schwieso, J. (1995) 'Tasks and tables: the effects of seating arrangements on task engagement in primary schools', *Educational Research* 37: 3.

Haviland, J. (1988) *Take Care, Mr Baker!*, London: Fourth Estate.

Haylock, D. (1994) 'The fruits of multiplying value', *Times Educational Supplement*, 2 December, section 2, p. 20.

Henderson, A. (1989) 'Multi-sensory maths', *Special Children* 33, 7–9.

Henderson, S.E. and Sugden, D. (1992) *Movement Assessment Battery for Children*, Sidcup: The Psychological Corporation.

Hinson, M and Smith, P. (eds) (1993) *Phonics and Phonic Resources*, Stafford: NASEN.

Hirst, P. (1974) *Knowledge and the Curriculum*, London: Routledge and Kegan Paul.

House of Commons; Education, Science and Arts Committee (1987) *Special Educational Needs: Implementation of the Education Act 1981*, Third Report from the Education, Science and Arts Committee Session 1986–87, vols. 1 and 2, London: HMSO.

House of Commons (1993) *Meeting Special Educational Needs: Statements of Needs and Provision*, London: HMSO.

Hughes, M. (1986) *Children and Number*, Oxford: Blackwell.

Hunter-Carsch, M. (1990) 'Learning strategies for pupils with literacy difficulties: motivation, meaning and imagery', pp. 222–36 in P.D. Pumfrey and C.D. Elliott (eds) *Children's Difficulties in Reading, Spelling and Writing*, Lewes: Falmer.

ILEA (1985a) *Educational Opportunities for All*, London: ILEA.

ILEA (1985b) *Improving Primary Schools*, London: ILEA.

Jones, G., Cato, V., Hargreaves, M. and Whetton, C. (1989) *Touchstones: Cross-curricular Group Assessments*, Windsor: NFER/Nelson.

Jowett, S., Hegarty, S. and Moses, D. (1988) *Joining Forces*, Windsor: NFER/Nelson.

Kelly, V. (1990) *The National Curriculum: A Critical Review*, London: Paul Chapman.

King, V. (1989) 'The practice papers: support teaching', *Special Children*, October, 33, 1–4.

Lawson, H. (1992) *Practical Record Keeping for Special Schools*, London: David Fulton.

Leclerc, M. (1985) *Classroom Aids, Apparatus and Materials*, Stafford: NARE.

Leicestershire LEA (1989) *Key Stages*, Leicester: Leicestershire CC.

Levey, B. and Branwhite, T. (1987) *The Precision Phonics Programme*, Stafford: NARE.

Lewis, A. (1985) 'Information skills for children with learning difficulties', pp. 27–42 in P. Avann (ed.) *Teaching Information Skills in the Primary School*, London: Arnold.

Lewis, A. (1991) 'Entitled to learn together?', in R. Ashdown, B. Carpenter and K. Bovair (eds) *The Curriculum Challenge: Pupils with Severe Learning Difficulties and the National Curriculum*, Lewes: Falmer.

Lewis, A. (1992) 'From planning to practice', *British Journal of Special Education*, 19: 1, 24–7.

Lewis, A. (1995a) *Special Needs Provision in Mainstream Primary Schools*, Stoke on Trent: Trentham.

Lewis, A. (1995b) 'The Code of Practice, the National Curriculum and children with special educational needs', *Education 3–13* 23: 1, 13–18.

Lewis, A. (1995c) *Children's Understanding of Disability*, London: Routledge.

Lewis, A. and Halpin, D. (1994) 'The National Curriculum and special education: a report of the perceptions of twelve special school headteachers', Paper presented at the annual conference of the British Educational Research Association, Oxford, September.

Lewis, A. and Sammons, P. (1994) 'The impact of the National Curriculum on children with special educational needs', pp. 74–87 in A. Pollard (ed.) *Look Before You Leap: Research Evidence for the Curriculum at Key Stage 2*, London: Tufnell Press.

Lewis, A. and Thorpe, L. (1989) 'Planning cross-curricular work within the National Curriculum, for children with learning difficulties', *Special Children: Primary Special*, pp. 5–7.

Light, P., Buckingham, N. and Roberts, A.H. (1979) 'The conservation task as an interactional setting', *British Journal of Educational Psychology* 49, 304–10.

Lindsay, G. (1981) *The Infant Rating Scale*, Sevenoaks: Hodder and Stoughton.

Lloyd-Jones, R. (1985) *How to Produce Better Worksheets*, London: Hutchinson.

Lloyd-Smith, M. (1992) 'The Education Reform Act and special educational needs: conflicting ideologies', pp. 11–24 in N. Jones and J. Docking, *Special Educational Needs and the Education Reform Act*, Stoke on Trent: Trentham.

Lowe, B. (1991) *Activity Sampling*, Hull: Humberside County Council.

Lunt, I. and Evans, J. (1991) *Special Educational Needs under LMS*, University of London: Institute of Education.

Lunt, I., Evans, J., Norwich, B. and Wedell, K. (1994) 'Collaborating to meet special educational needs: effective clusters?', *Support for Learning* 9: 2, 73–8.

McAsey, D. (n.d.) *Producing your own Educational Material, Unit 9, in Differentiating the Secondary Curriculum*, Wiltshire County Council.

McBrien, J. and Weightman, J. (1980) 'The effect of room management procedures on the engagement of profoundly retarded children', *British Journal of Mental Subnormality* 26: 1, 38–46.

McIntosh, A. (1978) 'Some subtractions: what do you think you are doing?', *Mathematics Teacher* 83, 17–19.

McNamara, S. and Moreton, G. (1993) *Teaching Special Needs*, London: David Fulton.

Male, J. and Thompson, C. (1985) *The Educational Implications of Disability*, London: RADAR (Royal Association for Disability and Rehabilitation).

Meadows, S. and Cashdan, A. (1988) *Helping Children Learn*, London: David Fulton.

Moore, J. and Morrison, N. (1988) *Someone Else's Problem? Teacher Development to Meet Special Educational Needs*, Lewes: Falmer.

Mortimore, P., Sammons, P., Stoll, L., Lewis, D. and Ecob, R. (1988) *School Matters*, Wells: Open Books.

Moses, D. (1982) 'Special educational needs: the relationship between teacher assessment, test scores and classroom behaviour', *British Journal of Educational Research* 8: 2, 111–22.

NAS/UWT (1991) *Teacher Workload Survey*, Birmingham: NAS/UWT.

National Council for Educational Technology (NCET) (1993) *Special Update (January)*, Coventry: NCET.

National Council for Educational Technology (NCET) (1994a) *A Software Guide for Specific Learning Difficulties*, Coventry: NCET.

National Council for Educational Technology (NCET) (1994b) *Access Technology: Making the Right Choice*, Coventry: NCET.

National Curriculum Council (NCC) (1989a) *Implementing the National Curriculum: Participation by Pupils with Special Educational Needs*, Circular no. 5, York: NCC.

National Curriculum Council (NCC) (1989b) *The National Curriculum and Whole Curriculum Planning: Preliminary Guidance*, Circular no. 6, York: NCC.

National Curriculum Council (NCC) (1989c) *A Framework for the Primary Curriculum*, York: NCC.

National Curriculum Council (NCC) (1989d) *A Curriculum for All*, York: NCC.

National Curriculum Council (NCC) (1989e) *National Curriculum Council (NCC) News*, December, York: NCC.

National Curriculum Council (NCC) (1989f) *An Introduction to the National Curriculum*, York: NCC.

National Curriculum Council (NCC) (1990a) *The Whole Curriculum*, York: NCC.

National Curriculum Council (NCC) (1990b) *National Curriculum Council (NCC) News*, April, York: NCC.

National Curriculum Council (NCC) (1992a) *The National Curriculum and Pupils with Severe Learning Difficulties*, Curriculum Guidance 9, York: NCC.

National Curriculum Council (NCC) (1992b) *Teaching Science to Pupils with Special Educational Needs*, Curriculum Guidance 10, York: NCC.

National Curriculum Council (NCC) (1992c) *The National Curriculum and Pupils with Severe Learning Difficulties*, NCC INSET Resources, York: NCC.

National Curriculum Council (NCC) (1993a) 'Pupils with special educational needs and exceptionally able pupils. Dissemination conferences 1993', Report to participants, York: NCC.

National Curriculum Council (NCC) (1993b) *National Curriculum at Key Stages 1 and 2: Advice to the Secretary of State*, York: NCC.

National Curriculum Council (NCC) (1993c) *The National Curriculum and its Assessment. Interim Report*, York: NCC.

NIAS (Northamptonshire Inspectorate and Advisory Service) (1992) *Planning and Managing the National Curriculum in Primary Schools*, Northampton: Northamptonshire County Council.

Nias, J. (1989) *Primary Teachers Talking*, London: Routledge.

Norwich, B. (1989) 'How should we define exceptions?', *British Journal of Special Education* 16: 3, 94–7.

Norwich, B. (1993) 'Ideological dilemmas in special needs education: practitioners' views', *Oxford Review of Education*, 19: 4, 527–40.

Norwich, B. (1994a) 'Differentiation: from the perspective of resolving tensions between basic social values and assumptions about individual differences', *Curriculum Studies*, 2, 3: 289–309.

Norwich, B. (1994b) *Segregation and Inclusion: English LEA Statistics*, Bristol: Centre for Studies on Inclusive Education (CSIE).

Nuttall, D. (1988) 'The implications of National Curriculum assessments', *Educational Psychology* 8: 4, 229–36.

Nuttall, D. (1989) 'National assessement: will reality match aspirations?', *Education Section Review, British Psychological Society* 13: 1–2, 6–19.

Nuttall, D. and Goldstein, H. (1989) 'Finely measured gains', *Times Educational Supplement*, 27 October.

OFSTED (1992) *Framework for the Inspection of Schools*, London: DFE.

OFSTED (1993a) *Education for Disaffected Pupils*, London: DFE.

OFSTED (1993b) *Access and Achievement in Urban Education*, London: HMSO.

OFSTED (1993c) *Assessment, Recording and Reporting*, London: HMSO.

Osborn, M. and Black, E. (1994) *Developing the National Curriculum at Key Stage 2: The Changing Nature of Teachers' Work*, London: NAS/UWT.

Pearson, L. and Quinn, J. (1986) *The Bury Infant Check*, Windsor: NFER/Nelson.

Peter, M. (1992) 'Editorial', *British Journal of Special Education* 19: 1, 5.

Peters, M. (1975) *Diagnostic and Remedial Spelling Manual*, London: Macmillan.

Pollard, A. (1987) *Children and their Primary Schools*, Lewes: Falmer.

Pollard, A., Broadfoot, P., Croll, P., Osborn, M. and Abbott, D. (1994) *Changing English Primary Schools?*, London: Cassell.

Pyke, N. (1995) 'Special needs tribunal confirms critics' fears', *Times Educational Supplement*, 27 January.

RDAMP (The 1981 Education Act: Research Dissemination and Management Project) (1989) *Developing Services for Children with Special Educational Needs*, Loughborough: Tecmedia.

Reason, R. (1993) 'Primary special needs and National Curriculum assessment', pp. 72–90 in S. Wolfendale (ed.) 72–90 *Assessing Special Educational Needs*, London: Cassell.

Reason, R. and Boote, R. (1986) *Learning Difficulties in Reading and Writing: A Teacher's Manual*, Windsor: NFER-Nelson.

Reason, R. and Boote, R. (1994) *Helping Children with Reading and Spelling*, London: Routledge.

RNID (Royal National Institute for the Deaf) (1970) *Hearing Test Cards*, London: RNID.

Roffey, S., Tarrant, T. and Majors, K. (1994) *Young Friends: Schools and Friendship*, London: Cassell.

Russell, P. (1990) 'The Education Reform Act: the implications for special educational needs', pp. 207–24 in M. Flude and M. Hammer (eds) *The Education Reform Act 1988: Its Origins and Implications*, Lewes: Falmer.

Rutter, M. and Yule, W. (1975) 'The concept of specific reading retardation', *Journal of Child Psychology and Psychiatry* 16, 181–97.

Sammons, P., Lewis, A., MacLure, M., Riley, J., Bennett, N. and Pollard, A. (1994) 'Teaching and learning process', pp. 50–73 in A. Pollard (ed.) *Look Before You Leap: Research Evidence for the Curriculum at Key Stage 2*, London: Tufnell Press.

Sawyer, C., Potter, V. and Taylor, T. (1994) 'Accessing the curriculum: how well do they need to read?', *Support for Learning* 9: 3, 120–5.

Sebba, J., Byers, R. and Rose, R. (1993) *Redefining the Whole Curriculum for Pupils with Learning Difficulties*, London: David Fulton.

SCAA (1993) *School Assessment Folder, Key Stage 1*, London: SCAA.

SCAA (1994a) *The Review of the National Curriculum: A Report on the 1994 Consultation*, London: SCAA.

SCAA (1994b) *The National Curriculum and its Assessment (Final Report)*, London: SCAA.

SCAA/OFSTED (1994) 'Letter to all schools, from R. Dearing and C. Woodhead', November, London: SCAA/OFSTED.

SEAC (1989) *National Curriculum Assessment Arrangements*, London: SEAC.

SEAC (1990a) *A Guide to Teacher Assessment*, Packs A, B and C, London: SEAC/Heinemann.

SEAC (1990b) *SEAC Recorder*, No. 4, Spring, London: SEAC.

Sedgwick, F. (1989) *Here Comes the Assembly Man*, Lewes: Falmer.

Shepard, L.A. and Smith, M.L. (1990) 'Synthesis of research on grade retention', *Educational Leadership*, May, pp. 84–8.

Shephard, G. (1994) 'Statement by Secretary of State for Education on Assessment and Testing Arrangements 1995', 5 September, London: DFE.

Shorrocks, D., with Frobisher, L., Nelson, N., Turner, L. and Waterson,

A. (1993) *Implementing National Curriculum Assessment in the Primary School*, London: Hodder and Stoughton.

Simon, B. (1988) *Bending the Rules: The Baker 'Reform' of Education*, London: Lawrence and Wishart.

Slavin, R. (1987) 'Ability grouping and student achievement in elementary schools: a best-evidence synthesis', *Review of Educational Research* 57: 3, 293–336.

Slee, P.T. (1987) *Child Observation Skills*, London: Croom Helm.

Solity, J. and Bull, S. (1987) *Special Needs: Bridging the Curriculum Gap*, Milton Keynes: Open University Press.

Stanovitch, K. (1994) 'Annotation: does dyslexia exist?', *Journal of Child Psychology and Psychiatry* 35: 4, 579–95.

Stott, D.H. (1978) *Helping Children with Learning Difficulties*, London: Ward Lock Educational.

Sugden, D. (ed.) (1989) *Cognitive Approaches in Special Education*, Lewes: Falmer.

Sugden, D. and Henderson, S. (1994) 'Help with movement', *Special Children*, 75 Back to Basics 13 (inset).

Sullivan, M. (1993) 'Suspended animation', *Times Educational Supplement*, June 4, section 2, p. 5.

Swann, W. (1988) 'Learning difficulties and curriculum reform: integration or differentiation', pp. 85–107 in G. Thomas and A. Feiler (eds) *Planning for Special Needs: A Whole School Approach*, Oxford: Blackwell.

Swann, W. (1992) *Segregation Statistics: English LEAs*, CSIE (Centre for Studies in Integration Education) Factsheet, London: CSIE.

Sylva, K. and Neill, S. (1990) 'Assessing through direct observation', Unit 2, Warwick University Early Years Team, *Developing your Whole School Approach to Assessment Policy*, Windsor: NFER-Nelson.

Sylva, K., Roy, C. and Painter, M. (1980) *Childwatching at Playgroup and Nursery School*, London: Grant McIntyre.

Tann, S. (1988) 'Grouping and the integrated classroom', pp. 154–70 in G. Thomas and A. Feiler (eds) *Planning for Special Needs: A Whole School Approach*, Oxford: Blackwell.

Tann, S. (1990) 'Assessment-led schooling? Reflections on term 1 of the National Curriculum for five year olds', *Early Years* 10: 2, 9–13.

Thacker, J. (1990) 'Working through groups in the classroom', pp. 68–83 in N. Jones and N. Frederickson (eds) *Refocusing Educational Psychology*, Lewes: Falmer.

Thomas, G. (1988) 'Planning for support in the mainstream', pp.139–53 in G. Thomas and A. Feiler (eds) *Planning for Special Needs: A Whole School Approach*, Oxford: Blackwell.

Thomas, G. (1992) *Effective Classroom Teamwork: Support or Intrusion*, London: Routledge.

Thomas, N. (1989) 'Letter', *Child Education*, October 5.

Tilstone, T. and Steel, A. (1989) *The National Curriculum and Severe Learning Difficulties*, West Midlands Monitoring group, Briefing Paper 3, Birmingham: Westhill College.

Times, The (1991) Editorial, November 4.

Tizard, B. and Hughes, M. (1984) *Young Children Learning*, London: Fontana.

Tizard, B., Blatchford, P., Burke, J., Farquar, C. and Plewis, I. (1988) *Young Children at School in the Inner City*, London: Lawrence Erlbaum Associates.

Todd, M. (1994) 'Squeeze tightens across the curriculum', *Times Educational Supplement*, August 26, p. 10.

Topping, K. (1988) *The Peer Tutoring Handbook*, London: Croom Helm.

Topping, K. and Wolfendale, S. (1985) *Parental Involvement in Children's Reading*, London: Croom Helm.

Turnbull, J. (1981) *Maths Links*, Stafford: NARE.

Turner, L. (1993) 'Special educational needs', pp. 137–57 in D. Shorrocks *et al.*, *Implementing National Curriculum Assessment in the Primary School*, London: Hodder and Stoughton.

Tyler, S. (1980) *Keele Pre-School Assessment Guide*, Windsor: NFER-Nelson.

Tyler, S. (1990) 'Subtypes of specific learning difficulty: a review', pp. 29–39 in P.D. Pumfrey and C.D. Elliott (eds) *Children's Difficulties in Reading, Spelling and Writing*, Lewes: Falmer.

Ware, J. (1990) 'The National Curriculum for pupils with severe learning difficulties', pp. 11–18 in H. Daniels and J. Ware (eds) *Special Educational Needs and the National Curriculum*, Bedford Way Series, London: Kogan Page/Institute of Education, University of London.

Webb, L. (1967) *Children with Special Needs in the Infants' School*, London: Collins.

Webb, R. (1993) *Eating the Elephant Bit by Bit: The National Curriculum at Key Stage 2*, London: Association of Teachers and Lecturers (ATL).

Wedell, K. (1990) 'Overview: the 1988 Act and current principles of special educational needs', pp. 1–10 in H. Daniels and J. Ware (eds) *Special Educational Needs and the National Curriculum*, Bedford Way Series, London: Kogan Page/Institute of Education, University of London.

Wedell, K. (1993) *Special Needs Education: The Next 25 years*, National Commission on Education, Briefing no. 14. London: NCE.

Wells, G. (1987) *The Meaning Makers*, London: Hodder and Stoughton.

Weston, P. and Barrett, E. (with Jamison, J.) (1992) *The Quest for Coherence*, Slough: NFER.

White, J. (1991) '"The goals are same" – are they?', *British Journal of Special Education*, 18: 1, 25–7.

Widlake, P. (1986) *Reducing Educational Disadvantage*, Milton Keynes: Open University Press.

Wiliam, D. (1992) 'Special needs and the distribution of attainment in the National Curriculum', *British Journal of Educational Psychology* 62: 3, 397–403.

Willes, M. (1983) *Children into Pupils*, London: Routledge and Kegan Paul.

Wiltshire Advisory Services (1992) *Policy into Practice*, Trowbridge, Wiltshire.

WO (Welsh Office) (1988) *Primary School Staffing Survey*, Statistics Bulletin no. 5, Cardiff: Welsh Office.

Wolfendale, S. (1983) *Parental Participation in Children's Education*, London: Gordon and Breach.

Wolfendale, S. (1989) *All About Me*, London: Polytechnic of North London/National Children's Bureau.

Wood, D. (1988) *How Children Think and Learn*, Oxford: Blackwell.

Wood, D., McMahon, L. and Cranstoun, Y. (1980) *Working with Under Fives*, London: Grant McIntyre.

Wragg, E.C. (1993) *An Introduction to Classroom Observation*, London: Routledge.

Wragg, E.C., Bennett, S.N. and Carre, C.G. (1989) 'Primary teachers and the National Curriculum', *Research Papers in Education* 4: 3, 17–46.

Yapp, N. (1987) *Bluff your Way in Teaching*, Horsham: Ravette.

Name index

Subject index

able children 4, 107, 112
accountability 17–18, 19–20, 53, 73
arts 27, 28, 36, 98, 99, 126, 170
assessment 6, 10, 11, 21, 24, 25,
    48–71, 116, 131, 133, 153–4, 160,
    168–86; curriculum-based
    64–70; diagnostic 65–70; SATS
    5, 25, 168–86; standard tests
    and tasks 23, 25, 45–6, 168–186;
    see also baseline assessment;
    Code of Practice; teacher
    assessment
attainment target 21, 24, 33, 35,
    36, 37, 39, 52, 54, 79, 81, 82, 84,
    95, 109, 113, 150, 151, 173, 189,
    194
autonomy 61, 118, 142, 144, 161–2,
    167

baseline assessment 48–54

caregivers see parents
child–adult conferences 65–70
clumsiness see developmental
    coordination disorder
Code of Practice 1, 2, 3, 8, 10–17,
    25, 35, 48, 54–7, 71, 88, 116, 125,
    130, 131, 132, 137, 139, 148, 151,
    152, 153, 156, 157, 167, 178, 197
collaboration: among children 24,
    31, 68, 98, 115–23; by teachers
    124–36, 137, 154–5; see also
    SENCO; support staff
confidence (in learning) 24, 31, 62,
    119, 142, 175–6, 180, 181, 182

continuing professional
    development 15–16, 62, 72, 75,
    130, 132
continuity 39, 78–86, 117, 146
coordinator for SEN see SENCO
cross-curricular elements 22–3,
    24, 38–9, 197–8
cross-curricular themes 23, 24, 27,
    35–8, 161
curriculum, broad 6, 8, 9, 21–34,
    35–47
curriculum audit 72

design and technology 27, 28, 36,
    39, 96, 97, 99, 113, 161, 170
developmental coordination
    disorder 61–2
differentiation 3, 6, 8, 9, 72–86,
    87–105, 108, 131, 175–7
disapplication 1, 18, 154, 187–96

Education Act: (1981) 5, 11, 18–19,
    153; (1988) 5, 20, 24, 26, 132,
    137, 140, 148, 188, 189, 194;
    (1993) 18, 55, 132, 148, 189
educational psychologist 39–40,
    125, 138
emotional or behavioural
    difficulties 17, 24, 138, 179, 189,
    190, 193
English 4, 25, 27, 28, 33, 36, 43, 70,
    79–81, 83, 84–5, 91, 95, 97, 99,
    108, 113, 143, 145, 157, 169, 170
entitlement 1, 6, 23–5, 187
equal opportunities 22, 73